MINIATURES OF FRENCH HISTORY

HILAIRE BELLOC

Sherwood Sugden & Company

PUBLISHERS

315 Fifth Street, Peru, Illinois 61354

DEDICATED TO
SISLEY HUDDLESTON

ISBN 0-89385-035-7

First printing of this corrected edition, 1990.

Cover: The Pantheon at Paris

CONTENTS

PROVINCES OR GOVERNMENTS OF FRANCE BEFORE THE FRENCH REVOLUTION

MINIATURES OF FRENCH HISTORY

THE FOUNDING OF MARSEILLES

(599 B.C.)

IT was the women who made Marseilles, and
through women did there first come to this
land writing and the living record of heroes, and
wine, and building with stone, and a knowledge
of the gods.

For the Phoceans, a Greek people from under
the sunrise, had sent forth (many hundred years
—more than five hundred years before the Romans came to make Gaul) a shipload to wander
and to find new land. But that ship's company
a matron of Ephesus had gathered together. She
was their priestess, and her goddess was at the
prow. And that women thus led had come about
in this fashion:—

The Phocean men having consulted an oracle,
the oracle had told them that they should send
to Ephesus, where great Artemis, the sister of the
Sun, had her temple and her shrine. So the

Phoceans sent an embassy to the shrine of the goddess, and while they were there great Artemis appeared in a dream to Aristarché, a matron of that city, and said to her (standing by the bed with her hands uplifted), "Take one of those statues which are sacred to me, and join you these Phocean men under their captain, Simos, and his son Protis, merchants, and sail with them to the new land."

The long Phocean ship, narrow and lithe in line like a greyhound, low in wall, shot forward under fifty rowers. She so roamed from headland to headland westward all the summer through, and her lookout peered for harbours that no man had yet taken, and for an open emplacement where the new city might stand. All the while the figure of great Artemis, the sister of the Sun, whom Aristarché served with sacrifice, stood upon their prow, and all their good fortune in the beginning of this thing was from women altogether. So they went on from headland to headland, still finding every place of vantage taken; and still shooting westward by day, anchored through the summer nights under the shelter of some jutting land.

Though they had so sailed for many days through the Mediterranean weather, they had not yet found a place for a city. Round the long bay which the Ligurians see from their high hills above the shore, round the bended knee of the north Italian waters, they found cities and islands and promontories encircling little gulfs, but none that would welcome them, and none standing empty for those who would seek new land.

Until at last, when they had passed and marked far inland to the north the high snows of the Alps, and when they had so divided the waters westward for many days more, they came to a shelter cunningly hidden by a god, but discoverable to sailors who had long known the sea. It was a place where many might pass and never guess an entry, but where one with keen eyes would discover, masked under a turn of rock, the gates of a harbour; and thither the helmsman steered them round with his broad oar astern, right round in a sweep (for the haven is cut backward, looking as it were not to the sea, but back again on to the land). And when they had passed the narrow gates they found themselves in a clear, deep pool with firm rock all about and riding for a hundred ships.

There did they let go the anchor, and came to rest after so long a wandering.

About the shores of this perfect harbour they saw no men, or houses of men, nor tillage of fields, nor temples of the gods, but very barren hills high inshore; and the place seemed theirs altogether.

When, therefore, they had landed, still under the guidance of the priestess Aristarché, and sent messengers up into the bare hill country and the low, spare brush of that land, those messengers came back to tell them that all this part was the country of a Ligurian king, and this king was friendly to strangers, and his name was Nam; nor had this people any knowledge of the sea, nor did they use boats and sails and oars, nor were they jealous of their port.

But first, before he would talk of anything with ambassadors, King Nam must give a feast; for he had a daughter to wed, and by the custom of her people she must choose her mate at this feast and declare him at the board. To this feast the Phoceans were bidden, and their embassy sat, with King Nam at his side, having for their chief men Simos the merchant, their captain, and the young man Protis his son; there also round the board sat the chiefs of the hill men, each from his tribe, for each was a suitor and hoped that King Nam's daughter would choose him. The name of that princess was Gyptis, nor did she come to

the feast where the men were, for she was a
virgin.

But when the feast was done and the time for
her entry had come, the king sent for the princess
and ordered that all should be done according to
custom.   And she came into the room like one
dreaming, and she held in her right hand a chalice
full of pure water, which she was to give to whomever she would, or to whomever the gods directed
her.   And that man to whom she gave it should
be her husband.

Gyptis then, going round the board while all
watched her, put forward the chalice in her hand
and held it out to the young man Protis, the
stranger from overseas; and he took it and drank,
and the king applauded, saying, "This thing was
done by the gods."   For it was a god that had
guided the virgin, and great Artemis presided
here, though the Ligurians did not know her, for
they were barbarians.

Once again, therefore, had the goddess worked
by a woman, and the chieftains from the hills
did not complain, for they knew her presence.

Protis, rising up and taking the cup, drank
from it and confirmed the espousals, and the
Ligurian men swore firm friendship with the newcomers, and granted them the shore; and, since

a harbour was their desire, King Nam made over this empty harbour to them, where the Phoceans, with great rejoicings and thanks to the goddess, built all that a city should have—a council-house, and a market-place, and walls, and gates, and a place for games, and a stronghold also upon a height behind the harbour, and temples for the gods. But their chief temple they raised to Artemis, and put in it that statue of her which they had brought from very far away, from the Phocean land and from home.

When all this was done, and the city founded and the harbour ordered, and ships sailing out and in, Gyptis and Protis, man and wife, were saluted king and queen of the city; but she queen more than he king, because it was the women that had made Marseilles, and they owed themselves all to the goddess.

Now when Gyptis and Protis had thus taken their thrones to rule over Marseilles from youth to age, they took new names as befitted their new station and the new fortunes of the Phocean land, and in these names they bore record of the great good that had happened. For Protis, the lucky bridegroom, called himself Euxenos, which is in Greek the "well fortuned guest"; but Gyptis, who had brought him so great a dowry, putting off the Ligurian name that her mother had given, put on a Greek name also, and called herself "Aristoxena," which is in Greek "the best of hostesses." And she worshipped with him her husband, and with all the Phoceans, at the shrine of Artemis, which Aristarché served, the priestess of the city. And so they ruled until they died.

This is the way in which Marseilles was founded, and thus it was that the women founded Marseilles.

THE FALL OF THE VENETI

(56 B.C.)

JULIUS CÆSAR had thought to have subdued all the country of Gaul and all the tribes
inhabiting it, and he had left in garrison, upon
this point and that, certain of his lieutenants with
their legionaries, while he himself went off to
another and distant part of his command—the
mountains of Illyria, which overlook the Adriatic
Sea; and this was in the winter, fifty-six years
before our Lord was born.

But during that winter time, when the gathering of food for the armies had made the Roman
officers in Gaul send out messengers and embassies
for the gathering of grain, the seafaring men of
Brittany, always in a way apart from other men,
and hard, and keeping their own counsel, and
difficult to subdue, had secretly prepared revolt
and had sent all up the Channel past by what is
Normandy to-day, and by what is the Boulonnais
to-day, and Ponthieu and the Artois, summoning
to their aid any of the sailors that would dare to
come, men knowing the rough seas, well pro-
visioned with many ships. They sent also over

the sea to Britain for aid, and from all these parts upon either side of the Narrow Seas they found alliances, for they were preparing a great thing. Cæsar, far off in the south, heard nothing of all this, and the great officers, his lieutenants in Gaul, were also ignorant of what was toward, so silently and rapidly did the Bretons work.

Until, as the year turned, young Crassus, who was in command over the Seventh Legion and had cantoned it for the winter in the country about the lower Loire, and who, like the others, had sent out his messengers to get wheat from the tribes around, heard that his embassy to the Veneti (by that name were these Bretons then called), Velanius and Silius, had been detained, and that the tribes farther on to the north in Normandy held also other deputies whom he had sent thither to levy food. Even as he heard this, young Crassus learnt from those whom the Veneti had sent to him with the news of their proud act, that if he would have his legates back he must himself give up the Breton hostages whom he had in his camp. Now these Bretons, the Veneti of Vannes, in thus detaining the Roman officers and in sending to their general such a message, knew that they had thrown down a challenge of life and death against all the power of Rome.

Out from that coast to the north and to the south of the Loire's mouth stretches for ever all away to the west the great ocean, here stormy beyond most seas and filling and emptying the rocky bays with swift irregular tides, and beating upon islands and many heaped boulders of stone that are islands at high water, and at low water joined to the mainland by spits of sand.

This sea the Veneti held, and they were the masters of it altogether, for though their own land did not reach to the Loire itself, yet their great ships were dreaded and obeyed for many a day's sail, and the rare shelters behind the juts of rock or within the islands they claimed to be theirs, even when the land about was tilled by another tribe. These great ships of theirs, which were their pride, stood up like castles out of the sea, very high at poop and prow, and of marvellous thick timber, with huge foot-square baulks and the nails clamping them thick as a man's thumb, so stout was all their building and so great and heavy were their ships of war. Iron also— and this seemed strange to the Romans and a sort of terrifying thing—were their anchor cables, and the vast square sails, whereby such weights of wood and men and iron were moved, were not of canvas but of hide, another thing monstrous in Roman eyes.

Against this power of theirs by sea the Veneti were very sure that the little men from the south could do nothing, cunning though they were in arts, and always favoured by fortune in their wars, and full of wealth, and coming—the leaders of them—from palaces for homes. For the Veneti were sailors, and sailors ever believe that the sea is wholly theirs, and is a certain defence against all evil and a certain avenue to all good fortune. But the Romans were soldiers, ignorant of the sea and fearing it, nor had they any fleet on those shores, nor could they seemingly make one which could at all dispute the mastery of the Atlantic with the great leathern-sailed vessels and their high freeboards that could withstand all the anger of the sea. And more than this, the Veneti knew what a labyrinth was all that coast under the water of it, and how many shoals and rocks there lay hidden by the tide, and where these lurked; and they knew what fate would befall vessels that struck, and they knew the shoals whereon their own great boats, flat in the bilge, could lie unharmed when the tide left them, but which would wreck hulls too deep and narrow, and ignorant of the peculiar custom of those waters.

To Cæsar, far off in the Illyrian mountains, this news had been sent by young Crassus post-haste, and he heard it as he was setting out to watch in Italy his rivals and his friends; for Cæsar, while he conquered Gaul, was thinking much more of how later he might rule Rome. He saw what peril lay to him and all his fortunes in this sudden pride of the Veneti, and in all this rising of the sailors who knew the Northern Sea from the Straits to the two Cornwalls. First he ordered, and that immediately, the subject tribes round about the Loire's mouth, and especially those who held the valley of the Charente and the harbours thereabout, and the men who lived upon the banks of the Loire itself, to build a fleet speedily and to send up such vessels as they had, that Crassus might have some weapon at least to his hand, and he sent up from the Roman shores —from the Mediterranean, that is—and from the Roman province which to-day we call Provence, rowers and men skilled in piloting, and a levy of the seafarers of the inland sea. But with all this he knew that he was attempting a doubtful thing, for his ships had no great strength, nor their sailors the skill of the Veneti, and their hulls were small and weak; and as for the Mediterranean rowers, they knew nothing of the Atlantic sweep, with its great rollers of Biscay under the south-west wind, nor of the heaving of the tides.

Next Cæsar, when he had laid his plans for Italy at Lucca, upon the road to Rome, came northward quickly into Gaul, and was himself upon these coasts of the Veneti at the moment when spring breaks over the wind-harried land and the wide heaths of the Bretons. And with his armies he laboriously worked up the coast, beleaguering first one stronghold of theirs and then another, but all the summer through (during which heavy storms broke continually, for that season was a wild one) he failed, and the Veneti kept him at bay. *They* could hold the sea in spite of weather; their stores and camps were on the islands and peninsulas to be approached only by the painful thrusting out of causeways from the shore, and when at last any one of these should be taken the sailor folk had only to put their people and their goods aboard and to sail to some other not yet conquered refuge.

Until he had the better of their fleet—if, indeed, he could ever hope to master it—Cæsar must despair of conquest, and with this successful stand of all the northern shores he would lose Gaul.

At last, towards the end of that summer, there

came a day in which his fortunes and those, therefore, of France and all the world were decided. For a gentler air was upon the sea coming up from the southward, and the Roman fleet, which wild westerly weather had kept imprisoned in the Loire for all these weeks, could clear at last.

It was upon a day when the sea was thus friendly, but the wind strong enough and steady to fill their sails, that the boats came out from the Loire mouth, making for the open sea.

There is in that country a great slope of open land standing above the sea and crowned by the old town of Guerande. And there, upon the low heights that leaned back from the sea and that overlooked islands and half islands upon the shore below and the harbour behind Croisic (where now the salt marshes are), lay stretched the Roman army, awaiting, helpless and as onlookers, the coming fight.

For as the light ships of the Roman fleet came sailing and rowing round the corner of the land, and appeared in procession upon the great open of the sea, from the harbour at the feet of the army the whole Venetian fleet, two hundred and twenty monsters, with their dark leathern sails and their enormous hulls shadowing the sea, stood out, with the wind upon the port beam, under that same weather, and marshalled in the open for the fight.   It was not quite noon.

Commanding those light, swift, but puny vessels upon whom his fate and that of all Gaul depended, Cæsar had placed Brutus, young, in his twenty-ninth year—Brutus, his darling, who was later to kill him in the Senate House at Rome. And this Brutus had designed, as his one hope against his enemy so greatly stronger at sea, something whereby he might board.   For the Roman was a soldier, and sure of victory with the sword.   This something was an armament in his light ships of long poles, to the ends of which were lashed curved blades—as our bill-hooks.   Against those high freeboards and against those tall poops the turrets which the Romans might run up upon their own decks availed nothing, and it was under the peril of a plunging fire from above and at the cost of a slaughter of which we are not told, that the southern rowers, bending violently to their work, shot up alongside of their great enemies, now two, now three engaging upon either side some one Venetian hull.   The hooks ran out and up, the blades caught the halyards, and the oarsmen, suddenly backing water, cut through those ropes cleated to the enemy's bulwarks; and here and there, all up and down the line, the Roman legionaries, watching from the heights upon the shore, saw the great leathern sails come crowding down, and the crew beneath them helpless. And everywhere the little southern men swarmed up the sides of the great Breton ships and boarded; and everywhere the sword conquered, though the long fight lasted through the afternoon under a wind that slowly died away.

Thus did Cæsar and his men see victory accomplished on the sea below them, before the sun had set over the calm to the west.

When all was lost, some remnant of the Venetian fleet not yet captured brought up their helms a-weather and stood to run before what was left of the southerly breath that evening into their harbours of the north. But the slight wind betrayed them, for before darkness it had utterly died away.

Thus was the issue of the Western world decided, and soon after all the land of the Veneti was in Roman hands, their great men put to the sword, and such of their people as had not fled sold into slavery, for a terror to all the other dwellers along the coasts of the sea.

THE DEATH OF ST. MARTIN

(*November* 11, A.D. 400)

WHERE the river Loire runs shallow or suddenly rising over its broad bed, broken by willowed banks of sand that stand above the summer stream and are, in spates, drowned up to their topmost branches; where it goes between sharp, low green hills on either side, wherein caves are a habitation for men; all down its valley by Tours there was a murmuring and a noise. It was November, and there were storms in the valley. The suddenly risen water drummed against the wooden piles of the long bridge of Tours, and was swirling brown and thick up to the lower branches of the trees in the islands. Nor could a boat go easily against it, though towed by strong horses.

Men were passing backward and forward to the north and to the south over that long bridge of trestles from Tours, the town, with its low roofs of spread red tiles, to the caves upon the farther shore, where was a hive of monks: all out of their cells to-day and eagerly hearing the news in the market-place. The very old man, Martin, the bishop of the city, was dying at Candes, miles away up river. He had not been able to come back to his own.

He was more than a king here, for he was also an ambassador of heaven, and when he had gone along the streets muttering to himself and blessing rapidly those who knelt before him, men felt that they had met not a man only but a spirit. The Emperor's Count who took the Pleas was small before him. The city held to Martin, and it was his own.

Its walls were filled not only with his long presence, but with the stories, grown greater through days of marching, of his strange missions into the eastern woods: into the Morvan, and the dark Vosges; and of dead men risen, and of lights seen in the sky. Also the army remembered him. He knew the quarters outside the walls where the huts of the barbaric soldiers were, and whence passed into and out of the gates of the city the gentlemen, their officers, marked upon their armour with silver and with gold. The soldiers had both songs and tales of Martin as he had been sixty years before, riding at the head of a column in his purple cloak; and those who had visited the German mountains and the valleys below the Danube could remember the portents of his birth.

Up there at Candes he lay dying, with some priests about him and the monks of a new house. He lay stretched upon a bed of reeds, still muttering to himself in a sort of sleep, the very old man. They watched for his passing as they stood around, and it seemed to them as though heaven was bending and touching earth to make a way for the ascent of his spirit.   All the Church of Gaul was centred here in his lean and broken body, and three full generations which had seen Gaul changed from the pagan to the Christian thing.   He still muttered faintly to himself upon his bed of reeds.

Within his closed mind, which no longer received the voices of this world, there passed great dreams or memories, and the perpetual wandering over the earth in the pursuit of his Lord filled Martin now, as he lay dying, with scene after vivid scene in which he stood outside himself and saw himself, and remembered all his time.

He felt, as his mind so wandered, a strong horse beneath him, and he was upon that western road which came up to the western gate of Amiens, straight from the Beauvaisis.   He was a young soldier; he was not much more than a boy. Against the metal scales of his jerkin the sword hilt tinkled as he rode; the air was keen with winter; there were dark clouds over the east, and a great menace of snow. The rolling upland was bare right up to the brick wall of the city. His mount moved impatiently through the biting wind, and as he went he saw, crouching at the gate of the city, that beggar man, the memory of whose eyes had filled all his life thenceforward. He remembered the look and how, with shame, but compelled by a fire within him (and looking up to watch whether the guard had noted an officer's folly), he had quickly cut his coat with his sword and thrown the fragment of warmth down to the half naked man. He saw—he saw the eyes still following him through the gate, not only with gratitude, not only with benediction, but also with prophecy, and he rode on into the town, ashamed in his mangled accoutrement, hiding the cut as best he could with his left bridle arm, but still thinking of those eyes. And Martin, lying there dying after full sixty years, murmured so that men around him could hear the words, "It was the Lord, Martin; it was the Lord."

Next he was in the deep woods of the Æduans,

high up in the hills, three days and more from posting-houses and from stone roads. The forest was damp all about him. He was in a clearing with two priests, his companions, and the wilder men of the hills were watching him sullenly while he broke their uncouth idol with an axe and preached to them the living God. But as he watched them he doubted their mood, and as he went back down the hills he feared their trapping him—even the chief whom he had baptized. Then all those trees quite faded, and he was in a place where the magnificence of the emperor shone—a huge figure, too strong and squat, with a bull neck corded, and the heavy, flushed face of exaggerated command. And he saw standing, richly clothed amid a group of clients, the eager, furtive, not sane face of Priscillian, and yet he pleaded for the life of that man. And lying so in his weakness and dying, his lips tried to frame the cry which came but as a whisper, though a whisper shrill within the soul: "The Church will have no blood. He is a bishop. The Church will have no blood." And again he was in the forum outside the palace wall at Treves, standing ashamed and with head bent, defeated, while the crowd came laughing and jostling by from the execution of the magician. He stood there alone and baulked, knowing that blood had been shed, and that he had been powerless.

Next, time rolled back within him, and he was but just free of his uniform, still so very young and full of his first fervours, and behind him were high mountains and about him the meres, the ditches, the reeds, the low lines of trees, and the hot sky of Lombardy. The straight imperial road ran right before him for a mile and more, and he limped along it at the end of his long, lonely journey towards the splendours, the high colonnades and the clangour of Milan. And even as he went, wholly bound up within himself and considering his mission from the Lord, he felt again that great fear which is not of this world, and which stands at last on the threshold of every death. His heart began to faint in him, and his thews were loosened, so that he could hardly stand. There was evil all around, and that awful presence of the Pit. Martin in his dream groaned and turned upon the reeds whereon he lay, so that the priests about him thought his agony had come. Within his mind he was still upon that Milan road, and still the oppression of evil grew, and still the dreadful mastery of the abyss and of things condemned. Then he heard once more right through him in its deep tones, as he had heard it then in his boy-hood, the challenge of hell, bidding him answer whither he was bound and what business he pur-posed to do. And Martin, as he lay dying, was again himself of those days, and found himself answering again from within: "Oh, thou foul beast, I go to do the work of my Lord." And again the mortal cold seized him everywhere as he felt, vibrating through his being, not heard by mortal ears, the mighty challenge of the receding ghost: "Martin, I will thwart you every way, and I will defeat you in the end."

The despairs seized him even as the scenery turned within his closed mind, and even here, in the article of death, the old man raised himself upon one elbow a little and stared all about. He had opened his eyes. He saw the room and the priests about him; one moved forward as though to touch him, but the others held him back. And a young man but lately tonsured, an Angevin from the valley, said with sobs, "Oh, my father, do you not know me?"

Martin, seeing that young face, smiled for a moment, but outwards only, for within the terror had returned. Though he now saw real men and the very walls of the stone room wherein he lay, and the true sky beyond the open arches, a November sky of driving cloud, yet was he in the presence of that terror, and he called out in a loud voice, challenging it: "Thou foul beast, I say to thee again, thou foul beast, what power hast thou over me? I have faithfully served my Lord, and I have done many and wonderful things for Him."

When the old man had said this so loudly, and while those about him were drawing back, many crossed themselves, feeling a combat of great power passing before them. They saw their father suddenly loosed from terror, and his limbs relax, and the falling upon his face of an awful dignity, which at the last relapsed into a stern but conquering smile. And so he lay backwards and was dead.

That evening they said Mass, and they absolved the body laid out upon a bier before the altar, and surrounded, as custom is, with lights, and the women also sang. And when the morning came they put the body of Martin upon a boat draped with hangings as fitted the greatness of the man and of his office and of all the evangelization of the Gauls. And certain skilful men having been chosen from among the river people to guide the boat over the turning of the flood water, they brought it down to Tours, and there they buried him amid a great concourse of the people, and all his monks lamenting him from the caves beyond the river. Then, when some years had passed, the devotion of his successors built a little chapel over that famous grave, and a bishop from foreign parts sent a sculptured marble for the tomb, and later still another church was raised in memory of the apostle. And one hundred years and another hundred years and another went by to the added glory of his tomb, until pagan savages of the north came and ruined it; and when it had risen again in splendour above him, other enemies, heretics, came and ruined it again, leavihg it all desolate and bare walls, and at last only two towers of what had been his shrine. But for the third time, and in our day, men built the shrine again, and there it is, as you may see it if you go. And so it will be, perhaps, for many lives of men to come—the Church rising and falling, and the tomb of Martin continuing in the midst.

THE BAPTISM OF CLOVIS

(December 25, A.D. 496)

THE great plains of Champagne were white
with snow, and the small rivers of that land
made little black ribbons across the desert of
frost. On the high hills that overlook the plain
from the west the deep forest of leafless trees
stood out as black against the sky in frost. The
town of those flats, all square, with its low
Roman walls and plain arched gates, was dark
against the snow in the midst of the level. The
straight arrow of the road making for the western
gate was dark also against the snow by the
passage of so many feet and of so many wheels
and horsemen, for an army had gone past.

It was in the Christmas time of the year 496.
The army was the army of that king from the
Netherlands, a leader of the Frankish auxiliaries
and their master in the forces of Rome. His
rough name of a Flemish sort his soldiers repeated
as Clodveg, or some such sound. For us and for
history it is Clovis, and there followed him in
that band of auxiliaries men, some of his own
small tribe which lay round Tournai and the

Lowlands, some from the Seine. Four thousand of them, perhaps: a column marching to his orders and ready to support his government, for government there must be.

Rome no longer truly governed.

Although these auxiliaries, like every other soldier, thought themselves Roman indeed, and were citizens indeed, and used the money, and when they could read could read only the letters of Rome; and though, apart from the army, all that world in town and country was Roman through and through, yet there went out now no orders from Rome to Gaul and the north. The sacred town was far. No tribute, though levied in the Roman name, went its way southward by the great roads to Italy. No writ came borne by a messenger to the Counts, each in his City.

Of that great body of arms which had been the pride and the sustenance of society there was now left nothing but these chance bodies, the auxiliary or regular, drawn from barbarian stock, fighting one with another each for its leader's command—and yet some one must govern. The money that passed with the emperor's head upon it (the head of the emperor far off in new Rome upon the Bosphorus) must be paid to an order, and some tax on it must sustain some chief who could settle between man and man and could put terror into wrongdoing, and confirm to a free man his brother's inheritance and the obedience of his slaves—yet there was still no government, nor any Justiciar in all these fields of Gaul. But the cities as best they could, jealously guarding their walls and arming their burghers for defence, stood each alone and kept their monies for their own chiefs; and the Counts, who once had been the officers of empire, lingered on: or stripped of power to the benefit of some greater citizen and wealthier, or still ruling, but ruling of their own right and with no charter from Cæsar: nor revocable, nor truly appointed.

For fifteen years all up and down the open country in between the woods, all up and down the old state roads still strong and hard, from city to city in the vague shocks of the time, this garrison that followed Clovis had triumphed. For Clovis the boy had led them first when he had come out of the Lowlands, barely fifteen years, and now, a man of thirty, he led them still. And it was with these his men never yet conquered that he had passed through that Christmas weather into the town of Rheims. He had come to assume government at last, and since Cæsar far away no longer ordered, to take up the business of ordering, between the cities of the north and among free men.

For now one hundred years had most men of the cities accepted the Faith.   And though amid the dwindling soldiery the gods of the pagans lingered, and though the auxiliaries, barbaric like the rest, followed, each group of them, the customs of the tribe whence it sprang, and for the most part did not yet know Christ, yet as they marched through that land they were marching through Christian land, and by this time the feasts of repose and the songs they heard and answered, and the rites of marriage when they would wed into the folk about them, and the rule whereby alone their children could succeed to their land when they had done with arms, all these things were Christian.   Stronger than the cities, much more real than the empty name of Cæsar, was the Church; and in each city a great priest, ordering the wealth of the clergy, administrating their wide farms and their thousand slaves, speaking with ancient authority and remembering Rome, ruled, and was a bishop.   Of these the greatest in that time was Remigius, whom we call St. Remi, the lord in Rheims and the father of Champagne.

This man, whose judgment and whose word

weighed much more with Gaul of the north
than many soldiers, had seen the young man
Clovis thus conquering to the east and to the
west, passing through the gates of the cities and
breaking in battle the Germans of the Rhine, so
that from the day of his victory no more hordes
came out from the forests, where there are no
towns, into the plains of Gaul. To the south, in
the name of Rome, there governed men who hated
the Catholic name and who had a pride in hating
it, because in the days when they had risen to
power and to be kings (each over his body of
garrisons, in the name of the emperor) the emperor's court itself had accepted heresy, and the
Catholic millions were despised. Here, in the
north, fate still hung doubtful who would seize
power, and, if he seized it, whether he should
stand with the bishops of the Church or against
them like the southern lords.

Clovis, three years before perhaps, had wed
Clotilde of great beauty and young, and for herself Catholic, niece of the Burgundian king; and
when their first son was born to them she had
him baptized as should be baptized the son of a
king (for Clovis was called "king" by the Franks,
the soldiers of his troop). But the child had died,
and in his death Clovis had learnt a terror of the

Cross. Yet was his second son also baptized with pomp, as though there were already about this warrior, his father, something imperial. And this second child lived. Then it was that in his battle with the German horde, out near the Rhine and in the thickest of the press when victory or rout hung even, Clovis made a loud vow to the God of Clotilde if he should be victorious over the Germans he would follow Him. He had won the victory, he had driven them over Rhine, and now at last with his men he was riding into Rheims for the feast, and Remigius knew that now Gaul, in the north, and as far southward as such armies could conquer, would be governed with the bishops and with the Church.

In the Basilica of Rheims, round-arched and long, Remigius ordered hangings of the richest dyes, come from the old time before the wealth and order of the empire had failed; and round the baptistry also he had the same colours displayed, and out of doors in the keen air across the streets of the town, and with pennons in the market-place, he ordered decorations as though for a victory. Pagan men come in from the hills understood the greatness of the moment. For all the history of France and the turning of it lay here, since Clovis, who must now take up government in the Roman name, and restore the fortunes of these cities, was to abandon the old and powerless gods and to be baptized.

They burnt incense in the baptistry on that short winter day, and lit a crowd of candles, making the round place glorious. But Clovis thought of the army, and before he would do so great a thing he appealed first to the soldiers (whom a chief must hold), lest too many of them should regret the old gods. But those who spoke for them bade him go forward, and whatever he did they would also do.

Then Clovis knelt for baptism amid those lights within, and Remigius, the great bishop, said over him not only the sacramental words, ". . . . of the Father, and of the Son, and of the Holy Ghost," which are the making of Christian men, but also those other famous words: "Bow down the head, Sicambrian, adore what thou hast burnt, and burn what thou hast adored."

When Clovis arose from the fount he had entered the company of Christian men. There were to be new things in Europe from that time and for ever, because the Gallic sword, which is the chief maker of Europe, had passed into the hands of a man so baptized. The proud heresies of the south were to pass at last, and there was to go out, even into the Germanies, where as yet were no cities nor letters, nor the art of building with stone, that influence from Gaul which has made of those forests an European thing. From this baptistry at Rheims set out a new story for the West.

As for the soldiery, these too for the greater part (three thousand of the men of his small army) were baptized when Clovis was baptized; and the new men to be recruited into the host for the new wars were to march henceforward in the Catholic name; and everywhere the peoples in suspicion of their not-Catholic lords, by the Alps as by the Apennines, by the Cevennes as by the Pyrenees, were to look to the north and to the Franks for their sword and for their deliverance.

THE BREAKING OF ISLAM

(October, A.D. *732)*

WHEN Christendom was Christendom at last, and all seemed bound together under one bond, the Emperor far in the East building his great Church, the Pope ruling in the West from Rome in the name of Christ, unseen lord of all Roman men; when Britain itself, swept by the pagans, was returning to the light of Europe, and when even in the Germanies, or on the edges of them, missionaries had begun to do their work, there had arisen, by that mischance which prevents perfection in any human thing, a new enemy far away in the desert.

In the hot sands of which Europe knew nothing, and which were for century upon century a boundary to all Roman things, in an obscure town free from Roman rulers, in a market-place of the Arabs near the Red Sea, there had arisen a man who was to change all. This was Mahomet.

Mahomet, acquainted with the Faith, selected from manifold Christian truth what few points seemed good to him, and composed a new heresy alive with equality and the reduction of doctrine to the least compass; rejecting mysteries—save that of immortality. He denied the Incarnation and left the Eucharist aside.

Mahomet had visions and heard divine commands. Stones spoke to him, and he perceived the glories of heaven. But more than this, in the desert places and under the brazen sun, he was filled with a command to teach what he had seen and known. He must re-make men. For this mighty task he found two mighty levers —brotherhood and simplicity—and to these he joined the delight of arms. For those who followed him were to be equal and to be brothers one with another, and this particularly as soldiers; and they were to spread through the world by the sword and by example the teaching that there was but one God, and that all subservience to men or to the forms of men, or the calling of a man a god, or the painting, or the drawing, or the sculpture of men, was an abomination. This something, simple, enthusiastic with the sword and proclaiming a binding equality, rose from the desert suddenly as its columns of sand rise in the whirlpools of hot air. It moved forth, as do those columns of sand. It came in a cavalry charge with Arab horses, and it conquered everywhere. All men who found it seized it gladly or submitted, and the great prophet was not dead a hundred years when this Arabian thing, riding out to destroy the Christian name, was hammering at Constantinople in the east, had burnt all through the African north, had swept Spain, had harried every coast of the Mediterranean Sea, had crossed the Pyrenees, and was striking at the heart of Christendom in Gaul.

Never had an issue so great been joined upon our western fields. Never since then, of all the great issues, has an issue so great been determined among all the great battles that our rivers have seen.

All Spain, I say, save the hills of the north-west, was held by this new power. Everywhere our shrines were subdued and our people despised, the subjects of these soldiers, when, from Spain as their base and possession, the Arabs determined to settle the quarrel for ever and to destroy the West in Gaul. It was the year 732 of the Incarnation. It was just a hundred years since Mahomet had died.

Across the high heart of the Pyrenees run, side by side in two gorges, two roads. The one is that which runs by the noise of the river

Aragon, and has above its summit the high peak Garganta; the other comes by the Gallego, and has by its summit the twin granite peak of the Midi. By these roads came, pouring over the high hills into Gaul, the myriads of the Arabs. And as they came they cried in every town of the plains that there was but one God, their God, and our shrines were desolate. They destroyed our harvest, they burnt our farms, they seized our citadels, they made still northward to decide whether the whole world should be Christ's or theirs. And Abdul Rahman, the viceroy, led them.

So they rode in their white cloaks, the thousands of them, on their light Eastern horses that were so quick of foot, and having on the thigh their short, curved scimitars, and slung at their saddle their small round shields. They came to the broad Garonne with its vineyards, and Eudes, the Duke of all that country, came out to meet them, and was defeated utterly. The walls of Bordeaux could not keep them out. They surged into that town; they burnt its churches also.

The broad Garonne was no barrier for them, nor the Dordogne beyond. They came up to Poitiers, and Poitiers first resisted. Its walls were too strong. Abdul Rahman burnt the

Church of St. Hilary without the walls, then left that hill town for a further attack when his triumph should be achieved, and led his myriads northward still on up the great road to Tours. For Tours was St. Martin's shrine and the heart of Gaul, and there should the doom of Christendom be decided.

There was in government over the armies of Gaul in that day a man called Charles, whom men also called "The Hammer." For many years had he warred with his men behind him against the other great ones in the north, for he was the bastard of the chief of the French who governed in the name of kings that were no longer kings.

This man Charles was forty-four years old, very strong and greatly dreaded, and all the things that the French had done in the old days he did, raiding in particular the Germanies, burning the pagan shrines in their forests, and taking tribute from the barbarians. Eudes also, in the south, he had warred against and defeated; but Eudes, now in this flood of the Arabs, called to Charles the Christian in the north, and Charles answered. He gathered universal levies from all the cities of the north, and from the valleys of the Loire and of the Seine, and from the edges of the Netherlands, and the forests of the east, and marched as though with a whole nation of men against the Saracens.

It was already autumn. Abdul Rahman was half-way come from Poitiers to Tours.

The place where his advance was halted by the coming of the French host is memorable.

It is a bare upland between the two rivers of the Vienne and of the Clain, lonely, with few hamlets, and in the midst of it to-day the ruins of a great Roman tower and the last traces of the great Roman road. There, in that autumn weather, the men scouting before the vast army of Charles found upon a Sunday evening the miles of tents, and saw the troops of horses picketed and the sheaves of spears, and rode back to the Chief with their news. There also in that bare plain, between the two rivers, which is to-day as deserted as ever, was the soul of Europe to be decided one way or the other, and the fate of the Christian name.

The Christian men came in their dense columns over the bridge where the rivers join. They poured into that peninsula; they also fixed their camp from stream to stream, and their great body of heavier horses, and their weapons, which were not spears nor scimitars, but the long sword and the long shield and the battle-axe; and they were summoned to the sound of horns and of great oliphants.

Now one day passed and another, and nothing was done; but at night each of the hosts could see the fires of the other, murky in the damp autumn weather, red against the low mists; and every morning, as the late sun rose beyond the valley of the Vienne over the damp fields of October through the fogs, the northern men heard the Arab call to prayer, shrill and singing, and the challenge to their faith and their name. And the Arabs could also see, far off across the space that divided them, men differently habited from the soldiers of Charles. They knew them well, for Spain was full of them. They were the priests.

So one day passed, and another and another, and yet no battle was joined; until at last a week had passed, and it was Saturday. Upon that morning, then, the leader of the Mahommedans, looking northward again to see what the camp of his enemies did, saw it covered all along its front by one packed line, dense, and cramped together as a faggot is cramped in its bond, all facing southward and hiding the tents behind with their line: for this was the army of Charles, now drawn up for battle.

There was a southern man, a Spaniard, who saw that sight, and who said that the men of the north were frozen men—men fixed by the cold with frozen faces, and he said that so standing all in line, not moving at all, they seemed to be a wall.

Then, before such a sight, the Arab army moved and swirled; there was the saddling of horses and the calling of the companies together with the shrill tube, and the words of the East cried from one to another, and accoutrement upon every side, until the light horses and their white-cloaked riders were ready, some with the thin lance levelled, some with the bared scimitar in hand, for the charge; and among them many wore mail, fine and closely linked, and iron upon their heads. But all were mounted for speed and for the rapid turning of a horse this way and that. The line charged. You might have seen the breaking of the white cloaks against those tall northern men, like the breaking of waves against a ridge of rock that bounds the sea. And when from that first charge they rode back, leaving the line unbroken, then one could see, scattered everywhere before that line, the bodies of men fallen, and of horses which the battle-axe had felled.

But again those thousands charged, and again

and with every charge lost more, not breaking the northern line. All the short autumn day was full of this fury and of these cries of the Orient, and of the scurry of hoofs; and throughout the full hours the men of Charles took the strain, killing and breaking the attack until, when the night fell, the assault had ruined itself; and in the counting of the dead they found that Abdul Rahman himself had fallen.

The night that followed so furious a day was a night of exhausted sleep. The army of Charles woke upon the morrow to see the day broadening before them over the plains still strewn with so many thousands of men and horses dead, and of wounded who had barely lived through the cold of the night.

As the early mist drew off they could perceive the Saracen tents still standing as widespread as a great town, but they heard no call to prayer nor any shrill trumpet, and they saw no horses at the cords. Charles's men were set out again for battle, but no enemy showed—only the dead. The columns were marched across the field, through the damp grass and stubble of it, all pounded into mud with the charging and the charging again of such hosts of horse. As they drew near, the skirmishers, riding ahead, challenged; but there was no reply; and as men passed for loot from tent to tent, finding all manner of wealth—blades damascened and jewelled in the hilt, and silks of Asia, cloths, and carpets and hangings, and ornaments of gold, and richly-painted parchments, the sacred writings of these desert men—they found no one alive save here and there some deserting slave who begged for mercy, or a wounded man still breathing, but too near his death to have followed the retreat. For during the night the wreck of that innumerable flood which had crossed the Pyrenees in the rising of the year had drawn back south hurriedly, leaving its train and its tents and its wealth to fall into the hands of the French.

Thus was Christendom saved in the tongue between the rivers, a little south of Chatellerault, and a day's march north of Poitiers; and if you go there to-day you will find the Roman tower still standing in a ruin, and a little village where the left of the Mahommedan line charged, called Moussais; and when you ask the people of the place what they call Moussais, they will tell you, "We call it Moussais of the Battlefield." So well does a peasantry remember after the passage of more than a thousand years.

RONCESVALLES

(Saturday, August 15, A.D. 778)

UPON the 14th of August, a Friday, in the
year 778, the Vigil of the Assumption, the
great host of Charlemagne was marching out
northward across the burnt plains of the Spanish
uplands to where, high against the sky before
them, stood the Pyrenees.

The Emperor that year had come down the
valley of the Ebro and had fought in that march
of Christendom against the Mahommedan. He
had held, but no more than held; and now he was
turning back home with all his thousands, and
with his great baggage train of loot and of provision, with his nobles and his prelates and his
barony, as it says in the song:—

> "Charles the king in a tide returning;
> Charles the king and his barony."

He was still a young man in the pride of life.
He was still full of his great business, which was
the restoration of the world and the pressing out
of Christendom by arms against the barbaric
German to the east, and here, though here only

44

in defence, against the Mahommedan to the south.

It was from Pampeluna, a Christian citadel which the Mahommedan could not hold, that the king thus set out to return over the passes to France and to the larger land—to the places where there was grass, and where the waters ran clear and brimming, after the treeless, parched mud and the empty torrent beds of Spain.

So the whole host went northward in its interminable column, mile upon mile. The camp that evening they pitched at the foot of the mountains; but the Basques all around watched them with spies from the hills, and envied so much wealth, and hated so many foreigners among them.

Before the next day dawned—Saturday the 15th of August, the Assumption—the vanguard was marshalled, and filed away upon the long straight Roman road that goes still upward northward into the summits, and when the sun rose it took full the limestone cliffs of Altbiscar, which are marvellous under the morning.

It was not till all those thousands upon thousands had gone their way, a cloud of dust behind them and the debris of their bivouacs, that a smaller body of the train, the rearguard, was marshalled to follow on. It had for captain and leader Roland, the Count of the Marches of Brittany, and with him were others of the Court —Adhelm, the chief of the royal table, and Eggihard. They had for their task that day to get over the pass and follow till evening the march of the main column. It was a matter, perhaps, of fifteen miles. Nor had they any warning of danger, for they were not in the enemy's country, and the last of the Emirs was two days' march behind them.

Where the Roman road between Gaul and Spain here crosses the Pyrenees, the sunlit side of it upon the Spanish southern slope rises most gradually towards the mountains, up a great shelving bank, as it were, miles broad and a whole countryside in length. It rises so gradually that men marching do not feel the strain, and an army has almost approached the limit of the ascent before it knows that the ascent has begun. For all that the shelf of land is lifted high into the air, and the notch, which is the Pass of Roncesvalles, seems, as you come on to it from the south, to touch the very plain. There is, indeed, just before that notch is reached, one little rise of less than a mile, which no man would take to be the passage of such mighty hills, so slowly and by so much cunning of nature has he been introduced to the high places. Here the woods are deep upon either side, and the last lift of the road goes up through greensward, very pleasant and cool after the dust of the plains. Before the rearguard, as the horses of its leaders took this rise, stood the edge of the saddle, clean marked against the noon sky—a crescent of wild grass sharply meeting the blue. It was when they had reached this height, Roland and his companions, that there opened before them the great sight of the gorge that plunges down, a passage into the Gauls and the larger land. Very far away to the north, a hazy line like the sea, framed between two distant mountain sides, was the level of the French flats and the Landes.

Down the sharp steep, on either side of the profound gorge, vast beech woods hung, falling in billows of greenery one below the other in the darker green of beech in August; such is for the solemn forest which clothes all that dark ravine, and from its unseen profundity there rises the noise of a torrent. This gulf is Roncesvalles. And down the western side of the awful valley, drawn like a thread through the forest, goes the old road, gradually lowering until, ten miles away and more, it comes to the waterside and to the mouth of these narrows at last.

By that road was the rearguard to go.

The noon woods in the hot summer weather were nearly silent. There was some murmur of insects in them, but no twig broke beneath the steps of a man. There was no hint of the many that watched and spied, hidden deep in the under-growth. The captains had loosed their helmets from their heads, they had hung them on the saddle-bows as the road went down through the beech woods; the shadows were cool. And the companies of the rearguard sang in the ease of the descent, and the drivers on foot were guiding their beasts, for the way was narrow and pre-cipitous to the right, where the ground sank to the torrent below. One hour and two hours the column so went forward, with nothing about it, as it seemed, but the silent mountain tops—the bare rocks lifting up above the green of the forest, and the noise of the torrent always nearer and nearer as they went downwards.

There is a place in Roncesvalles where the gorge singularly narrows and the steep sides become precipitous cliffs approaching one to-wards the other. Here also the old road has come down to some few hundred feet from the torrent bed, and as the head of the column reached this place the sound of the water was much louder in their ears. Roland and his peers, remembering Spain, were refreshed, for now at last they were in the gateway of the Larger Land —the *Terra Major,* Gaul, their home.

Here, where the ledge of the road passes through the defile above the river, it also turns, so that a leader looking backward does not see more than some few yards of the column following him. It was in this place, in the Pass of Roncesvalles, in the mid-afternoon I think (seeing how their march was planned), that the disaster broke.

First came bounding down in longer and in longer leaps from the rocky ridges, thousands of feet above, one great boulder. It sprang over the way, missing men and beasts and wagon, but striking confusion and fear. They heard it crashing in the woods below them, and breaking through the bushes and splashing into the water at last. The column was halted and bewildered. There were horses thrown back upon their haunches and wagons slewed across the way, and angry calls from the leaders to disengage the block, and the bunching up of those marching on from behind, who had not seen what happened. Upon such a confusion came a rain of smaller stones (but stones that could kill a man), bounding down the mountain side. One team was swept away, its wagon toppling after it, its wagoner pinned beneath. One file was cut right asunder, and the cries of those crushed under the weight of the rock made echoes from side to side of the gorge.

There was a little pause in which one heard the shouting of the officers to rearrange the line, and mixed orders for defence in a place where no defence could hold. Then from the far side of the narrows, from the dense wood of the opposite steep beyond the stream, came the whistling of an arrow, sharp, utterly new, meaning men and men enemies, though not a face was seen. It struck a captain's horse behind the shoulder. The beast squealed and reared and threw its rider, and then, still staggering upon its hinder limbs, fell backward over the steep and was caught in the sharp edges of the wood still screaming. That first arrow was a signal. There came at once a flight of others, and another flight, and another. Men fell crawling upon every side, and the narrow way was a surge of them struggling for cover where there was none, or trying to climb over and around their fellows and to hide beyond the bend. Into the midst of the welter came a new discharge of the great stones from above, and then with a sort of universal cry (all the rearguard of Charlemagne's host being now confused and hopeless) the forest awoke, the hills were full of voices: and the Basques were upon them.

Roland of the Breton March, riding at the head of his command far down the road and well past the bend, had heard the first cries of distress and the first turmoil. He had thought that some blunderer had lost his wagon down the steep, or that the column had received one of those checks which, in marching down a narrow way, bad management will give. He was for riding back at first when, at a place where a level of grass breaks the rocky steep and leads away up from the road to the left, to the heights above it, he saw issuing out from the woods before him the press of the mountaineers. With him was his guard and certain of his peers.

Before the shock came upon him he had looked down into the road, which he could well survey from such a place, and he saw in a moment what had come. He saw the summer sky of the afternoon, blue but misty above them, and the deep forest which had been so silent all about, and he saw, high in heaven, between the peaks, one great bird and then another, slowly circling upon black wings. And he saw the whole body of the rear-guard stretched out upon a mile of the way, of the narrow way, and everywhere dark masses of men not in the accoutrement of the host, livelier, striking with knives, not sworded; and perpetually, as men fell, and as traces were cut and teams destroyed, these enemies would leap off into the undergrowth again laden with booty. All the while there rang in that echoing place cries in a tongue he did not know, and that no man knew —the Basque tongue, the oldest tongue of the world. And urging the mountaineers on and on, in rush after rush from the heights, in charge after charge from the depths, was the little bagpipe of the mountains, screaming its war scream —the little bagpipe of goatskin, with its two flutes which the mountaineers threddle with their fingers, while their eyes gleam. That was what he saw—the destruction of all for which he stood responsible to his young king, who, in the plains below, had already camped his great army after the passage of the mountains.

Men see such things manifold and disastrous in one manifold and disastrous moment; and Roland had seen this in the moment between his reining up upon the sward above the road and the charge of the mountaineers against him. He drew the two-handed sword from its sheath; he had not time, nor any of his companions, to helm; but in some hope of succour, or in the determination to die, he formed them into a little square against the onrush. But even as they formed they were borne down. The mountaineers were upon them in a hundred, and then in a thousand, stabbing with the short knife, and with three men to take the place of one who went down under the long sweep of the sword, delivered heavily from the saddle.

The beasts were stabbed down, and the riders, as they fell heavily, stabbed upon the ground. It was a swarm of foot against few horses that destroyed that knot of captains. Behind them the resistance had almost ceased, the column was extinguished. Among the dead and the dying, and the horses now no longer plunging but still and fallen, the derelict wagons, full of the loot of Spain and of the provision of so great a host, stood gaping for the robbers. The mountaineers climbed with odd laughter up the sides of those wooden things, and passed one to another, quarrelled over, fought over, ivory and gold, and good wines, and salted meats, and hangings and stuff for tents, and cloth of the Saracens, and spices.

When evening came on there began to draw away from that place of death the thousands who had so triumphantly designed the surprise, and the wreckage was left in Roncesvalles under the open night, with its leaders lying dead round Roland, and their mounts dead also upon that little place of grass beside the road.

They say that not one man escaped from the slaughter of Roncesvalles to the main army, and to Charlemagne and to the Larger Land. But this cannot be so, for from that dreadful place there went forth at least such men as could tell the story and make it greater, until there rose from it, like incense from a little pot, an immortal legend which is the noblest of our Christian songs. Therein you may read the golden story of Roland—how he blew the horn that was heard from Saragossa to Toulouse, and how he challenged God, holding up his glove when he died, and how the angel took him to the hill of God and the city of Paradise, dead. And as the angel so bore him Roland's head lay back upon the angel's arm, like the head of a man in sleep.

THE NORMAN SIEGE

(Winter, A.D. 885–886)

JUST as the hard winter had closed right in, and the days, growing shorter and shorter, were bitter under the silent cold, and all the trees were bare, there came, rowing through the chill and swollen water, and past the leafless forests of the western hills, up to the very water chain of Paris, such a fleet as had not been seen before. There were seven hundred at least of these broad ships of war, strong enough for the seas, small enough for the rivers, and they had so come slowly up the stream from Rouen, which had fallen that summer to their arms. Everywhere, as they went thus slowly inland week by week into the winter, the banks had flamed with farm fires, and the fields had been ravished and men and women killed, for this great host and fleet were the host and fleet of the pirates.

They were not Christian men. They knew nothing of the rule of Rome. They came for destruction and to loot and to enjoy, and they were barbarous. Before them all the land had bent, and yet they could make nothing—only war.

Men watching this dreadful thing when day fell upon the 24th of that November in the year of 885 of our salvation missed the glint of light from the water. All the Seine was covered with their ships, and with the more numerous barges of their provisions and their arms, right away from this water entry into Paris to the western hills. And at first it seemed that God Himself could not have saved the city. For the suburbs upon the northern and the southern bank, upon either side of the island whereon Paris stood, were open and undefended, and though all who could pour into that small island were huddled there behind the shelter of its wall, and were armed for the defence of the bridges leading to the Island-City from the north and from the south, there were only two towers or works to support the resistance—that guarding the northern bridge, called the Little Castle, and that to the south, called the Tower of the Little Bridge.

Within the city the monk Abbo watched all, and he has written it down in verse for us. Nor was what he watched a small thing. Here was, with Paris, France and all Christendom in the balance; and this swarm of the empty northern savages about to extinguish the light.

Within, to defend the city, was first of all the

Count Eudes, the son of that Robert the Strong, the founder of his line, who had fallen at Brissarthe, and beside him Gozlin, the bishop's and Gozlin's nephew Ebles, the abbot of the great Abbey of St. Germans outside the walls, all good bowmen; and under these the Parisians were to make trial which should win—the little fortress of Christendom or the black north.

When the barbarians had moored their vessels and established their camp, and beleaguered the city all about, they made a great charge to enter by the northern bridge, and strongly shook the Little Castle which defended it. But they could do nothing against it, for the defenders threw down fire upon them, and the best of the fighting men were there. Also there were perpetual sallies from within. Count Eudes, the lord of the city, rode out with his spear, and coming back with pagans upon it, said, "I have game upon my spit." And when the assailants, tortured by the thrown fire, threw themselves into the Seine water, the citizens mocked them from the walls. But the assault was fierce, and Abbo in his tower heard even by night the whistling of the arrows.

Upon the fourth day, when this assault had failed, the northern men withdrew and were content to make a great camp over by the Abbey of

St. Germans to the south of the city, and to wait until they had further prepared.

Then it was that you might have heard sawing and hammering all the short days long in this camp, and seen great felled trees brought in by wagons for the fashioning of the engines of war. The night fires also of their feasting glared right into the city, and all the suburb round about was burnt, and the church and the monks also, but the bridges and their defending towers still stood, nor could the host of the pagans yet strike into the Island City itself.

Two months thus passed in the working of the winter wood into engines for the siege, until at length, with the end of January, upon the last day of that month, the assault upon the Little Castle of the northern bridge was taken up again: this time with all the new things—the towers, and the catapults the pagans had fashioned; and in particular they had with them a great ram which they had made. Swinging it with repeated blows, they shook the wall, but still they failed. And on the next day, and the next—that is, upon the eve of the Purification and upon the day of Candle Mass itself—they still thundered at the wall of the Little Castle, but they could not take it. Only once their great ram made a breach, and those packed men within saw the northern men without, all helmeted, and these, seeing the armed men within, stayed and did not charge. In the night that breach was built up again.

Then, the three days' battle thus lost, the northmen thought, since they had so failed against the northern bridge, to try the southern, where a smaller tower was. For they were like wolves that prowl round a house in winter, nosing to find if any latch has been left undone, or they were like the north wind of winter, buffeting a house and seeking some way in.

It had so happened that in this same week of Candle Mass the melting of the snows up in the Morvan, under a breath of milder wind, had swollen the Seine high, and the flood of it had carried away the piles of the Little Bridge to the south, and had left it in ruins; and so the tower beyond it, which defended it, and the twelve men within, were left all alone. These the pagan host, having come round to the southern bank after their defeat upon the north, challenged and summoned, but they would not yield. Then the pirates, seeing that this little band of a dozen were beyond succour, and that none could reinforce them, piled wood all about the tower and set fire to the wood, so that the stones cracked and crumbled, and that the beams within and the roof were aflame. The twelve men within were forced out by the fierce heat, but yet they would not yield. They got them backwards upon the ruined ends of the bridge, and there, drawing their swords, they prepared to meet any that should come against them; though they knew that this was useless, for now there was no defence left to flee to behind them (the bridge being broken down) and many thousands of the pagans before, since the tower had fallen. The pagans therefore summoned them and offered them life, and they, upon promise of their lives, came up on to the land; but when they came there the pagans, who were treacherous, killed them in spite of their word. And the Christians upon the walls of the city saw this thing done beyond the river.

There was in Paris a certain man of great birth and wealth, and one of the leaders of the people, who had heard the perpetual cry of the citizens against the Emperor, that nothing was done for their relief, and that they must die un- succoured. And this man escaped by night and went off eastward to find the Emperor Charles where he might be, and to bring him to shame, for if Paris fell the northmen would ravish all Gaul, and Christendom itself might fail. The bishop was dead of the siege; spring had come, and yet there was no message of relief, but still the block of the invaders and a perpetual defence of the bridges. One duke, indeed, whom the Emperor had sent, coming with a column, had fought his way in with food; but there had come no strength to disperse the host and the fleet of the pirates, and once again the city was beginning to starve. Therefore did this man of great birth, and a leader, leave the city to find the Emperor, who should have succoured Christendom; and the man who thus left to shame the Emperor into marching was Eudes himself, the lord of Paris.

He found his Emperor Charles surrounded by his Court at Metz, whither he had marched back from Italy. The Emperor Charles was huge and unwieldy of body, and he was palsied so that his head shook, and he had no will. But Eudes spoke to the Nobles and shamed them into marching, though it was not until July that they tardily agreed to go westward, nor until September, when for now ten months little Paris had stood up against the northmen, that the great army of the Empire was seen marching up from the north and the east, until it lay camped below Montmartre, not an hour from the town. Even here so feeble was Charles that he would not fight when he saw the host of the northmen. He lay there in his camp treating, and one that watched him has written: "He did nothing worthy of the Majesty Royal." And it was October, and nearly a year since the Normans had come, before his treating was ended.

The chief of the pagans was one Siegfried, who had sailed from Thames, having gathered his men about him at Fulham above London, after King Alfred had broken their power. Siegfried it was who had so sailed with his followers out of Thames mouth and up Seine, sacking Rouen and coming at last to Paris itself. And with Siegfried the dull, palsied Emperor bargained, buying him off with silver to seven hundred pounds weight, and shamefully permitting that heathen to go east into the heart of Gaul and to pillage Burgundy.

So was the great siege ended and Paris saved by its valour and by the valour of Eudes: but not avenged, because the blood of Charlemagne had lost its vigour in his descendants, and the Emperors were nothing worth.

But as for Paris and her lord, they now stood out separate from these Emperors who could do nothing for them; and Eudes, the son of Robert, made himself more great, so that when Charles the Emperor died a year later, the great men met together and said to themselves: "As for the Germanies, let them go where they will, but Eudes shall be our king here." And Eudes was crowned and anointed in Compiègne, not two years after his manliness in the great siege, and being so crowned he rode out eastward to where the northmen were pillaging in Argonne, and finding there the body of the pirates he destroyed them; and to this day it is remembered how powerfully he blew his horn in that fight.

From him and from his father Robert all the kings of France descend.

THE CROWNING OF THE CAPETIAN

(Sunday, July 3, A.D. 987)

LET any one who would understand the fortunes of the French wander for days in the wooded valley of the Oise. There great forests still clothe the low rounded hills which border the widenings of the slow river, where it saunters through its pasturages and its marsh, with tall, delicate aspens in solemn lines to mark its passage. It is a flat river floor of half a league across and about it the great woods of Compiègne and of Coucy, and all the others that still bear the name of their towns or castles, make a sheet of trees. That sheet of trees may have been a wider thing in the old days, but it remains for any one who will visit it (and it is a countryside that will harbour a man for as long as he will, so broad is it and so deep) the memory of that landscape in which the fortunes of his country changed and re-arose.

But, in particular, the forest of Coucy and the depths of the tall trunks understand how the lords hunted there when the Emperor was still the Emperor, and before France was once again

France. See how there still remain in fragments the lines of the Roman roads that led from town to town; all the towns that make up this countryside. Consider Paris, one hard day's ride away, two or three days' marches. Remember Laon on its impregnable horse-shoe hill upon the edge of those woods, overlooking the plains to the east and the north, and forming a bulwark and a stronghold for the last of the blood of Charlemagne.

Then, in your mind, see westward and southward the open land, Normandy and Anjou, the Island of France, the gardens of Touraine, Nevers, the high Morvan, the Champagne, crammed with Latinity, and the valleys of the Allier, of the Cher, and of the Vienne, leading upwards and southwards into those dead mountains of the centre which are the frontier against the south. Remember also the good lands that flank Brittany, and that make an approach and a barrier at once for that jealous, silent land. Do all this, and you will understand what happened when the Carolingians fell, and when, in one moment, a new line of kings that stood for Gaul re-arisen was accepted and crowned in the person of its ancestor.

France would be. The Germanies learning the Faith, and informed by the French, were still the Germanies: barbaric, lacking in stone and in letters; lacking in roads. The Latin speech had not followed in them the Latin rule, and the Church which had made them human had hardly welded them into Christendom. It was not possible that Gaul should any longer be confused with these, unless, indeed, they would consent to be ruled from Gaul. That, in their new-found faith and culture, they would not consent to. Yet the imperial line and the old name of Charlemagne, now wasted for nearly two hundred years, pretended to control the issue. But France knew itself again—that is, Gaul knew itself again, through the confusion of how many centuries, and a symbol must be found for France. The line of Charlemagne was exhausted. It could present for claimant to universal rule over the Germanies, as over Gaul, as over Italy, nothing that men respected, no one whom soldiers followed.

But in Gaul itself was a family and a man.

That Robert who had died at Brissarthe, and who had come, no man knew whence, but who was so strong, and who was called "The Strong," had founded lineage. It was a man of his blood who had held Paris against the Normans. Men of his blood had claimed the crown and kingship once, and had been a part of the Empire, and had yet dropped the claim. But their great estate of land had grown and grown. Their command over many soldiers had grown therewith. They spoke in the Latin tongue; they were of us. And of all of those who were of us they were the richest and, what is much more, the most captaining family of them. Of that great line Hugh was now the man. For a hundred years his father and his father's father and his father before him had been the true masters of those good river valleys, the Loire, and the Seine, and the Oise. If there was to be government, he, Hugh, must come.

Rheims of the Champagne, the town where Clovis, five hundred years before, had accepted the Faith and made a unity for Gaul, had in this moment for its great archbishop one Adalberon, a man very subtle, and more learned than subtle, stronger in will than either in his learning or in his subtlety, and perceiving future things.

In those days there was between men a division. The great were very great. The mass of men were hardly free, and were all very small. The slaves that had worked for Roman lords in generations now half-forgotten, if they were no longer slaves, were still mean men; and the few that could ride by the day through their estates

inland were great above all men—the great bishops, the great counts, the men of the palace, and
the masters of the countryside.

These, then—the Empire now plainly in de-
fault, and wealthy Gaul, as it were, derelict, and
the Germanies, in their barbarism, sheering off—
counselled what they should do. They met in an
assembly, going up the northern road from Paris
to Senlis; and here there was great tumult. For
each man came with his armed men about him,
and confusedly they knew how mighty a thing
was toward.

In that tumult it was Adalberon who spoke:
"Charles of Lower Lorraine," he said, "has many
to speak for him, and he says that the throne
should come to him by right of lineage. But
there should not stand at the head of this kingdom any but he who is great. Hugh, the commander of armies, is known to you by his deeds,
by his descent, and by the armed men in his
troop, who are many. If you will have government, take him."

In the further tumult that followed Adalberon
persuaded, and Hugh, coming from those who
had saved Paris, and who had commanded armament in Gaul for now so long, was acclaimed by
the great lords as king.

When the time came for the anointing and the crowning, and for this separation of France again from what was not France, this re-seizing of the nation to itself, Noyon was the town they chose.

Little Noyon, with its vast arcaded church, strong and Roman, amid the woods of the Oise, the altar before which Charlemagne himself had been crowned. To Noyon they came in the midst of those forests of the Oise, by that strict road of the Romans which bridged the river, and which is but one of the many that there meet, as in the centre of a wheel; for the dignity of Noyon, now so forgotten, lay in this—that men could come to it easily, even in those days of difficulty and of old arts forgotten.

In Noyon, then, was Hugh crowned.

He had no name but Hugh. Since, however, men must give names to a family as well as to a man, all the generations after him have remembered what his nickname was. For he had a nickname, this soldier and lord, and from his helmet or his hood he was called Hugh Capet, the man of the head covering—the man of the head or cap. And that is why this family is called Capetian: a little cause for a great thing.

THE TORRENT

(A.D. 1030)

DOWN the mountain side there went in long
procession, slipping here and there upon
the unbroken frost of the morning, jangling all of
them with bells, mules by the hundred—quite
three hundred mules.

They that led them were short, lean men with
hard, clean-shaven faces, bronzed in colour, and
on their heads they wore a loose, flat cap that
hung to one side or the other. Each man led
his beast, and each beast was heavily laden as it
picked its way down the slope; and here and
there, sitting sideways upon her mount, was a
woman of these hills, holding in her arms a child.
The sun had not yet risen behind the red earth
of the eastern peaks. The broken road that had
once been a passage for the Roman armies over
the Pyrenees (and that was now a mere bank,
unsurfaced, down which the mules warily shuf-
fled) was touched everywhere with rime. For it
was but the opening of summer, and the snow
still lay everywhere upon the high mountains
around.

At the head of the valley below, fixed in the narrow valley floor, lay huddled and tangled together such a little mass of dirty brown as looked like a fantastic chaos of rock. As one came closer one could see that it was a cluster of human buildings—a town, but a town so squeezed together, so suspicious of all around, so made for defence, that, seen from the pass above, it was like the shell of some armoured animal.

One street alone led through its houses, very narrow indeed (for up in these mountains nothing goes on wheels)—so narrow that two loaded mules could barely pass. And this narrow street, under the first glory of the morning sky, which made a strip of light above it, was full of the cries of sellers and of grooms, of the stamping of horses' feet, and of the innumerable little jingles of steel which come from bit and bridle and curb, stirrup and scabbard and halter-chain, and the rings of mail upon a hauberk, wherever men are gathered together to ride out in arms.

For there was in this town an assembly made of farmers and free men and one or two lords as well. They had come for the beginning of the summer season, now that the crops were sown, to ride out south against the Mahommedan, to see what they could see, and take what they could take. It was for this force that the mules were coming over the hills to provision it. A great train did every such expedition need of servitors, and oats, bread twice baked, and salted meat tied tightly round with strings, olives also, and oil and much wine; four men, perhaps, afoot for one that fought on horseback; and many of those afoot were half slaves.

Under the low, thick arch, where the track came in through the town wall and became the narrow street of the town, swayed in the first of that long procession of mules. To the cries of the sellers and the grooms, and to the jingling of steel links, there was now added the music of little bells. But dominant over all such noises, louder than them all, and a background of sound upon which all this life was woven, was the torrent swollen with the melting snow that ran beyond the houses a few yards to the east, and filled the deep, cool valley with its rumour. The name of this torrent was Aragon.

Near a wide and ancient door of mouldering oak, that hid a deep, dark stable beyond, was a farmer from the Canal Roya upon his horse, and he talked to his lord.

"Those of Jaca, at the beginning of the plain, sent in a man last night to say that we could catch a few of them beyond the Peña, beyond the high hill. They camped on the slope of it, marauding. We should be upon them before the sixth hour. It is not many miles."

But his lord, looking at the Peña where it stood, a grey wall miles away, answered him,—

"Their horses are swifter than ours, and they go very light without armour, God curse them!"

And he spat as he spoke of the Moslem.

Then the farmer said,—

"Two days ago they raided the farm of Peter, the free man, and took his four serfs away on halters, running behind their horses, and they burnt a rick of his, and behind them they left a coin. This coin I bought of Peter."

He showed it. It was a coin of the mint of Saragossa, and the lord bent over his saddle and peered curiously at the Arabic script stamped upon it. Then he made the sign of the Cross slowly over his broad shoulders.

"These words," he said, "are in the devil's language, and with these they summon Mahound."

"Sir," said the farmer, "some day some men now mounted here will ride into Huesca and cleanse it of the infidel. There is a monk who lives alone, and is a hermit up on the Peña. The

Mahommedans fear him and will not pass his cave, and God gives him knowledge in dreams. This man is very old, and this same Lent he said (when he came down into Jaca for the Adoration of the Cross and the Blessing of the Oils), this very Lent he said (and from the altar, note you, by leave of the bishop), that he had seen St. Lawrence standing glorified in the air, who held a banner, and that Huesca would be ours and Christ's at last."

The lord smiled. "These things are lies," he said.

"Was not Huesca the town of the great St. Lawrence," answered the farmer doggedly, "whom the Emperor of the Romans, possessed by a devil, roasted upon a gridiron for the Faith? Will he not lead the host into Huesca at last? And then all the plains will be before us, whereon we can call upon St. James, and charge!"

But the lord still shook his head and smiled unpleasantly.

"All these things are lies," he said. "But whatever great lord shall ride at last into Huesca for Christ, and cleanse it of the infidel, shall not only conquer it for Christ but for himself. Sancho is our great master, whom we serve, but whoever can hold Huesca will be a little king all the same."

The farmer looked back up the narrow street to the mountains, and he said, "The lords come riding in from the Major Land, from the broad Christian land that goes up and away northward for ever beyond the hills; they come in greater and in greater bands with every season; they are strong men heavily accoutred. With their aid we shall take Huesca."

"But this season," laughed the lord again, "we shall not take more than a farm, nor raid more than an orchard, nor carry much home beyond a few apples, and a little wheat perhaps from the first plough lands of the infidels in the plain."

By this time it was full day. There was a new warmth in the air, and the noise of the torrent seemed louder under the growing light. The torrent, roaring southward, seemed, with its adventure and its plunge, a sort of leader; and these mounted men, now gathering into column for the raid, thought of the south and of the stony path that led along its banks on, away, over the ford to Jaca: and thence to the plains and the battle. The torrent of Aragon is a maker of kingdoms and of soldiers destined to conquer. Though as yet these Christians had but a few bare parishes of land, hardly held by day and by night with arms, and the little town of Jaca only for their bastion, yet in them all, whether doubters or visionaries, there lay smouldering some certitude of future things, and a promise of the reconquest of Spain beyond and of the freeing of all Christian land.

So they rode out, in number about four hundred and fifty mounted men, with many more afoot that made a straggling herd about them and behind them. So they filed out by the southern gate.

The priests and the women watched them as they went by, and so did the children in the crowd. There were shrill cries of prophecy and of warning. To the last of them that rode by a deacon held up the relic of St. Lawrence, which was a piece of cloth from his tunic. The armed man bent over the saddle on the near side and kissed it as he passed.

Their marching raised a cloud of dust that blew softly away to the southward under the summer air, and in a little while the noise of the horses' hoofs was lost, and the little place was quiet again.

There was a woman, one of those that had ridden in with the mules. She stood now by the fountain filling a leathern gourd with water and crooning a song of the Basques. For she was of the Basque country, to the east, an unconquered tribe. And with her was her little son, four years old, who held her skirts and watched the cool, clear water running into the gourd.

"Mother," he said, "where do all those tall gentlemen go?"

"They go to fight against the men in white cloaks," she said, "the men who serve Mahound. They go to catch them in their camps, and to bring us home good things—as it says in the song that we sing on winter evenings," and she crooned the tune to him.

The little child said, "Mother, what is Mahound?"

"Mahound," said the woman, "is a great beast that lives in an island of the sea. He has a head like a goat, and great shining eyes."

The child looked at her, glorying and delighting to hear the story again. "And are not his eyes jewels?" he said.

"Yes, baby," said the woman, "great jewels from the East, such as there are in kings' crowns, in the crown of Sancho our king, or in the middle of that cross which the archbishop bore before him in the procession when he came down this Lent from Toulouse with the great lords of the north who were riding to help Leon."

"And mother," went on the child again, "is

there not a fire behind those eyes of Mahound, and has he not great gilded horns, and does he not prophesy from his goat's mouth?"

He continued to recite all the tale that he knew so well.

"Yes, baby," said the mother (the gourd was filled, and she was leading him away by the hand), "and this beast is black all over, whence they that worship him, the Moriscos, are dark also, and they grin with white, shining teeth like his. And between him and his followers and our Christ and His Blessed Mother and His Saints there is perpetual war."

As the child so babbled, and as the woman answered him, there still ran, with its triumphant noise below the houses, the thundering torrent. The little child caught between two walls the glint of its water foaming under the sun.

"Mother," he said, "what is the name of that water?"

She answered in a more solemn tone, "Its name is Aragon, a famous water; the sick bathe in it and are healed, and from all time it has baptized Christian men."

*　　*　　*　　*　　*

When this child was grown a man, though he

was a serf's child he became skilful in the riding
and the management of a horse and in the handl-
ing even of arms, which the young free men lent
him for a jest in the village games. So at last he
went riding as a companion with one from his
village, and was enfranchised. And by the time
that he had taken his farm from his father and
had himself bred a son, he followed the Cid
Campeador. At last he, too, grew old. He came
back to his farm to sit by the fire; and his son
in turn tilled the land of those few acres in the
hills, and rode out every season farther and farther south against the oppressors, cleansing the
land. Until there came the rumour of a great
marching that was going eastward to the Holy
Places for the recovery of Christ's grave, and this
son of his, following that rumour, begged of his
old father a little store of gold which he had put
by, and went out himself upon Crusade, leaving
the old man by the fire in the Pyrenees.

THE CONQUEROR

(January to September, A.D. 1066)

WILLIAM, the Bastard of Falaise and Lord of all Normandy, had ridden into St. Germer four days before the feast, and with him a small retinue very richly dressed.

Upon the day of the feast he stood in the ante-chamber of the presence near the chapel door with but two to serve him, which two stood behind and were humble, the one a clerk, the other a treasury man but a knight. Normandy had on the sword belt and the sheath, but not the sword. For it is not lawful to carry arms in the presence of the crown.

William the Bastard of Falaise, thus standing in the ante-chamber of the presence by the chapel door, was taller than his servitors, yet he looked short, so round and bull-like was his head, with its close-cropped dark hair, and so broad his neck and shoulders. In that close-cropped dark hair one could see already lines of grey like steel, for the man was in his fortieth year.

The two guards that stood before the curtains of the arch moved backwards. An old man, dressed in the long tunic of a civilian, which was embroidered everywhere with thread of gold, pulled back the cloth, and William, striding through, saw beyond, upon a chair that was carved and gilt for a throne, Philip, the boy who was his lord and his king, yet no older than one of his own sons. The boy's face was heavy and not courageous, but his eyes had in them already that look of patience and of knowledge which had built up the royal line.

William, Duke of Normandy, designing to conquer England, desired from his soul to have all France behind him, and secure peace while he was abroad: therefore had he come to the court of this boy-king of France, his relative, to offer him the shadow of suzerainty over England while he should grasp the substance of power in London. But the boy-king had been warned and was old enough to understand the ruse.

William, the Duke of Normandy, knelt on the second step of the throne and took the boy's hands between his hands and kissed his finger tips. Then he rose and spoke of his petition. England was his of right, and he would seize it as of right with his companions; but he would not hold it against his lord, he would hold it for his lord. Such things already Philip had seen in the parchment, and he, William, Lord of Normandy, had come to hear the answer from the king's mouth. The boy shook his gold-circled head very gently, but did not open his lips. Said William the Bastard, Lord of Normandy, "You are my lord and I am your man, but, a little way from here, where there are men that are my men and a land over which, under your allegiance, I am lord, my armies are ready, and from my treasury I shall have hired others from the east and the west, and even from Touraine, and there are strangers from the south that will sail with me; and if God grants me this kingdom, I will not hold it as king—God forbid that I should make myself equal to my lord. Therefore the headship of this island (if God gives me victory) is for you to take, King Philip, as a child may pick up a toy."

Now when Duke William used these words "as a child," King Philip smiled with his lips drawn downwards, and nourished revenge in his heart; for he knew very well what the great vassal meant, and how he had cast a net to bring in the power of all France in aid of him, and to have peace behind him when he sailed. He knew also, by wit of his own and by councillors, that whoever sat in Westminster beyond the sea could laugh at writs from Paris, and therefore, relaxing that smile of his and looking, though not courageous, stern—almost as though he were already a man grown—Philip refused again.

William, the Bastard of Falaise, Duke of Normandy, rose from his knees and looked angrily about him, at the servitors of the Court and at the guard, as he would look at equals, and even at the king he looked as he would look at an equal, thinking, perhaps, that with others to aid him he might dethrone that boy. But saying nothing more, he bowed as a man should to his lord, and turned and strode out again beyond the curtains; his clerk and his knight of the treasury, that had stood there for witnesses, following him.

Then he got back into his own land, to Rouen upon the broad Seine, where the woods are so deep for hunting all around; but he was for hunting things that do not live in woods, and for a ride into a farther place than the domains of the Caux country. And in those woods for many a month men were felling timber and bringing the green baulks in creaking wagons to the slips of the Channel shore, to Caudebec, and to Quillebœuf, and to Honfleur, and to the river that is below Caen—to all the places where men build ships upon the sea marge of the Normans. And for three months or so he was summoning by writ his men and their men's men, and by letters with promise of pay and of booty he was getting from off his western March the sad Bretons, and from off his eastern March the pale Picards and the Lowland men. Until at last he had in Dives mouth a very great fleet of vessels large and small, the largest so large that fifty knights with their horses and all their men could cross the sea thereon, and the smallest boats of four fathoms long, not even decked, and stowed to the bulwarks with casks and stores, and the garnered oats of that year's harvest, and wheat and little mills for grinding.

Men came to him from over the sea telling him how Harold laughed at his claim. William, the Lord of Normandy, watching the sea from the cliffs of the Caux country, found it still angry day after day and week after week, with the cold north-east wind blowing strong upon the land, so that he could not venture, and when he did there was shipwreck; but his mariners lay apart after the mischance, waiting orders, until at last he bade them beat up the coast to the great and wide bay of the Somme, where stood his Port of St. Valery, half sheltered from the gale.

Now some days before the Feast of St. Michael, in that same year, the strong cold wind from the north that had blown so long died down at last, and the sea heaved only and did not break, and a warmer air came up from the south-west, like a piece of summer again. So that, upon St. Michael's Eve, Duke William put all that great host on board, his fifty thousand men and his many knights, and his horses and his provisions, and in the afternoon, the tide making outward from the bay, all his hundreds of boats set sail, making a cloud together upon the sea, and all that night, under the lighter breeze, they ran for English land.

When the morning broke, which was St. Michael's Day, they saw, high and white in the dawn, the great cliff jutting forward, behind which was their harbour; and one hour and another, as the sun rose, those miles of sails drifted forward upon the flood eastward to behind the lee of the head until, in the third hour of the day, the square walls and the bright red roofs of a town stood close before them, and inland beside them a great sheet of water, shoal, but with fairways known to mariners, and a narrow entry from the sea; and this was Pevensey Haven. Then the men, looking out from the baskets on the mastheads of the great ships, called to the helmsmen below to shift the helm by this board and by that, that they might follow the fairway in. The smaller ships were beached within, all along the level sand, until at last, what with the greater vessels lying secure at anchor, and the lesser ones drawn up in rank beyond the high-tide mark, all his fleet was still and his great host made land. This was the way in which William, the Bastard of Falaise, Duke of Normandy, came with so many thousands to the kingdom of England, which he would win.

THE SERFS

AT Marmoutier the monks St. Martin had lived now for seven hundred years, the lords of much land. Before their ancient caves in the rocks, which had been their cells and which ran into the low cliff to the north of the river, stood now great buildings of stone. A vast church was there, round arched, enormous, heavy, and a great gateway with its gate-houses, upon the summits of which men had carved two angels, the one blowing a trumpet and the other sheathing a sword. And all around were barns and further buildings, the habitations of the monks, and their cellars, and their kitchens, their great hall, their place of account.

In this last, the place of account, in a smaller chamber apart, whose window without glass took in the full sun of morning, sat three clerks, monks of Marmoutier, two young, one old. Now the old one was the procurator, and his name was Augustine, for he was called after that saint; but the two others were in the service of the accounts, wrote at his bidding, and found for him what was owing and upon what date, and from whom, whether in money or in service, throughout all the wide lands of Marmoutier that were its dower. Of these two young clerks the youngest, who was but a novice, still bore his name in the world, which was Raoul; but the elder, who was already a priest, had now his name in religion, which was Leo.

They were nearly at the end of their business and at the last of the lists, for the morning was far gone, and very soon the bell would toll for the chief meal. Outside the air was filled with the scent of hay, for it was summer and the time of mowing. There was a noise of scythes far off. It mixed with the running of the river.

There was a difficulty and a doubt. The old procurator, Augustine, in the place of accounts that day had a troubled face, desiring to do right by young Walter (Reginald in his father's name), a keen possessor, loving the land of his mother and his home near the monastery of Marmoutier. For on that farm called Hauterive, in the good pastures behind the dykes of the Loire, there was uncertain custom, and upon the same land service to two lords, the monastery and this same Walter (Reginald in his father's name).

And the procurator would not decide until he had spoken fairly with that lay lord.

For with the wealthy villeins upon this wealthy farm (which was full four furlongs of the river side) all along the Loire it was a custom as old as the woods that they should serve their lords upon Monday and Friday. So much was sure. But there was a division among them, some coming to the castle gate and some to the monastery gate; and in the time of Reginald, who was cunning and not just, some had gone to the castle who should have come to the abbey: which was a wrong. But now that Walter the young man, the heir, had possession (his father just dead), they could make a firm pact together, the monks and he, and each have his due of labour, for Walter was mild and equable; and also it was here at Marmoutier that he had learnt as a boy the Seven Arts, and the Psalms as well.

When, therefore, he came in (which he did without retinue) the old man greeted him friendly, and they sat down to the pact.

But still there was issue between them upon these wealthy villeins of Hauterive.

"Brother Raoul," said Lord Walter, "what now is written down?"

"Give me the parchment," said Father Augustine, the procurator. Then he said, "My lord, there is but one sentence as yet written here and the beginning of the next, but more cannot be written until we know that you will sign."

Then the young lord said, "Read me what is written that I may hear." And the procurator read out,—

"We, the monks of Marmoutier and Walter, Lord, hold in common sundry serfs, men and women, now to be divided between us in severalty. Therefore at this present, being the 6th day of June, in the year of the Incarnation, 1087, and Bernard being abbot, we have proceeded to the division of the men children and of the women children of——"

Then old Father Augustine looked up from the parchment and said, "My lord, until we have agreed, it can go no further."

Walter, the young lord, rubbed his shaven chin with his hand, and looked sidelong at Novice Raoul. For Novice Raoul, being the son of one of the villeins adjacent, could bear witness.

Brother Raoul spoke,—

"The farm which my father has in villeinage marches, Father Procurator, with Hauterive farm, and as a boy, before I came to holy service here and to the special following of God, my father and I, on those two work days of the week that are due to the lord, went in company with those of Hauterive, who were more wealthy than we from the goodness of their land; and I can bear witness to custom."

"Of the elders," here said the young lord, "there is no question, for I freely allow what Abbot Bernard has written me and Father Procurator here—to wit, that Renaud, whose house is called the 'Village House,' is due for the two days' labour at the monastery gates, and Guascelin, the other villein upon Hauterive land, is due at the castle gates."

The monks nodded, agreeing.

"We have but to agree upon the children, their dues of labour, as they come to that age when the custom of the manor demands it. This must be settled."

"So we have set it on the parchment," said Leo, the monk who had not yet spoken. "So we have set it, lest, when they grow older, quarrels, as in the time of your father, should arise."

Then the Father Procurator spoke again,—

"If Renaud of the Village House chooses to redeem in coin, we shall settle it upon our admitted rule, Lord Walter—two-thirds to the monastery, one-third to the castle."

"That would be but just," the young man assented.

"He will not redeem!" broke in Novice Raoul quickly.

"Surely," said his colleague Leo mildly, "he is rich enough! It is the best land on all the river side, and there are one hundred arpents of it, and it has a vineyard too!"

But Raoul laughed, remembering his father's neighbour.

"Yes, the Serf has money lent out; but for that very reason will not Renaud of the Village House redeem. For he loves the very metal. Also he has other labour of his own cotters on his land. And when his children grow up and pay their dues of labour days, Renaud will be glad to see them go to the monastery gate or to the castle gate, though he lose their arms and hands for that day, for he will say to himself, 'There they go a-saving of many pence in redemption, and their food also this day they will have from the lord, or from the abbot.' He will not redeem! He will in no way diminish his hoard!"

"See now," said Father Augustine, who waited every moment for the bell and was weary of this long business over a small thing—"see now, if we admit this rule of a third the matter is

quickly settled, for this Renaud has six children—
two sons and four daughters; Guascelin three, or
four if you shall count a very young child still
in her cradle."

When he had said these last words they all
laughed, thinking of the baby and of what hay-
making it could do. Then the young lord, to
save them further delays, rose as to agree.

"Read me the list," said he, "and take you
in the one the first four names, in the other the
first two. As for the one that is in the cradle,
she can wait;" and at that they all laughed again.
"It will be many years before we need speak
of any labour in our fields from her. Perhaps
she will wed out of villeinage, or perhaps with
her portion she will farm free land, or perhaps
she will be a nun. So engross the matter thus,
and we will have secured peace and a settlement
between us."

Then Brother Raoul carefully wrote the square
letters with his pen, adding, "We then have received for our lot of the children of Renaud of
the Village House one boy, Bartholomew, and
three daughters, Hersende, and Milesende, and
Letgarde. And of the children of Guascelin one
daughter, Aremburge, and one son, Walter. A
very young girl child in her cradle is excepted

from this allotment. She shall be between us, if she lives, until some settlement shall allot her to one or to the other lordship." And with that his writing was done.

With these as witnesses, the procurator set the abbey seal, and Walter his seal also and the mark by which he was known, and so was the settlement concluded, just as the bell rang for the prayer and the chief meal.

Outside in the warm air the noise of the scythe ceased to the sound of the bell, and there was nothing heard but the gentle wash of the river running by its bank of reeds—the broad river Loire, low in the summer drought, and showing above its streams of blue water white sand-banks sparkling in the sun.

JERUSALEM

(*July* 15, 1099)

IT was Friday, the 15th of July, in the year of
the Incarnation, 1099, and about noon. A
little sun stood right up in the height of heaven,
blazing as no sun shines upon our tempered and
well-watered lands, for it was the sun of Syria,
a burning eye.

The rolling upland was brown and bare,
scorched for weeks; the harvest long gathered,
and all grass for forage lacking. Across its sweep
rose a little town of tents, deplorable with use,
torn, patched, and dirty; at long cords stood
tethered the lean horses, their heads patiently
drooping in the heat, and here and there a gap
where one of them had fallen and would not
rise again. Beyond the camp a dusty, winding
track, very wide, just marked by shallow ruts, led
away to the horizon and to the crest against the
northern sky, whence could be seen, very far off
to the westward, the Levantine Sea. Along that
faint, broad line ominous wreckage was studded
at intervals too close—carts broken down, glis-
tening white bones, and little heaps of refuse

which hid the dead. Of the millions that had marched out from Europe three years before to the rescuing of Christ's grave, a handful were here, still breaking against the long, low wall of the city. Of twenty that had left the pleasant fields at home, in Picardy or in Touraine, from the Garonne, from the cool flats of Vendée, but one had lived or had persevered to see Jerusalem. And now for all these days the last effort had still been quite unavailing. But it was Friday, the day upon which Christ had died; it was noon, the hour of His Crucifixion.

In the camp, which looked southward towards the low wall of the city, the serfs were now painfully bearing water up from the stagnant pools below, or were attending the fires for the cooking of meat, against the hour when, once again, as for so many days, the armed men should come back at evening sullen and once again defeated; from that camp, I say, the serfs could see, all along the wall, the assault proceeding. Beyond, within the city itself, glaring in the intense light, was the low, whitewashed dome, the Sepulchre, and Golgotha was just before.

It was by groups that the desperate attempt was made, as it had been made day after day during that intolerable heat of the Eastern summer. One could see little figures running with the short scaling ladders, bucklers lifted in a tortoise to shield the bearers; the ladders rapidly put against the wall; men swarming up, now one group just getting a foothold, but soon thrust back again; bodies falling, heavy in their armour, to the ground; the ladders here and there along the half-mile of front broken or thrust outward, and whole lines of men that had mounted them crashing again to earth. While underneath the wall, cowering close in the dead ground, free from arrows above, were other groups that fiercely picked the ground with their steel, and that thrust into the gaps faggots to which they would set fire. The smoke rose, blackening the stones, but none crumbled, and there was no breach.

In two spots near either end of the line great beams had been mounted, swung on ropes from tripods, and these, with regular thud, pounded at the lower courses of the huge blocks that built up the rampart; while in one place a tall scaffolding, or tower of wood, having upon its every tier a hundred archers and slingers, poured missiles down upon the defenders of the battlements.

Far off as the camp was, one could hear above the regular pulse of the battering rams a noise like that of the assaulting sea in a storm when it bursts upon the shore and when the shingle screams under the retreating wave. And the high calls upon the God of Islam, which for now so many months and years had rendered a haunting sound in their ears, pierced through the general din. Voices were calling also from the minarets.

Very far away to the south, beyond the whole expanse of the city, could just be seen a squat, strong mass of masonry overtopping the houses. It was the Tower of David. And there these men, who were so fiercely pushing the assault from the north under so intolerable a strain of heat and clamour, knew that the men of Toulouse, the southerners under their Count, were pressing and besieging also. For beyond that Tower of David, higher than it and feathery against the sky, was yet another tall scaffolding of poles lashed together, black with tiny figures of the Christian soldiers, shooting down upon the defence and attempting to master its fire. But of that distant struggle no rumour could be heard; there could only be seen the general movement of men against the sky.

The general tide of this assault upon the northern wall perpetually repulsed, perpetually returning, sounded hour after hour. Noon was

past, and the seventh hour and the eighth. The
dust of the conflict had already mellowed the light
of the sun, which no longer stood in the zenith,
but was partly declined. The time was near
that ninth hour when Jesus had cried out that
God had forsaken Him, and had dropped His
head and died.

The men watching the camp, the serfs, listless
in their fatigue and broken by the noonday heat
now past, thought they heard a new note in the
distant noises from the wall. One looked up, and
another, and there was almost eagerness in their
gestures. Those with keener eyes pointed to a
place a little east of the centre of the line, where,
as it seemed, a blacker and a denser mass was
gathering. It was like a swarm of bees. They
saw the little figures racing up to join the edges
of the rapidly swelling mound of men. The many
ladders there concentrated were hidden beneath
this cloak and moving garment of human bodies,
and the whole surface of it running upwards in a
slope to the very height of the battlements glit-
tered and twinkled, like beaded stuff, with the
points of steel, with the steel caps, and with the
little bristles of swords ever mounting .

The camp was afoot, every serf was standing
and looking. The wounded, such as could still

know their names or the place in which they lay, such as could still move, were warned by their servants in the excitement, and crawled to the gaps of the tents. Such labourers as had fallen asleep were roused and stood, in their turn, straining their eyes at the wall, and one or two in their eagerness began to run forward, unarmed as they were, across the brown, burnt earth between the camp and Jerusalem. Was there a breach? There was no sign of it. No crash of boulders, no sudden rising of that cloud which booms up as from an explosion when a wall gives way. The regular thud of the battering rams continued far to the right and far to the left uninterruptedly, but between them this climbing, struggling, increasing mass of men gave forth a louder and a louder note. They were upon the edge of victory.

Then in one critical moment (it was just three o'clock) the desperation of those cries turned into a very different roar of cheers, and it was apparent that the wall was gained. One could see the besiegers spreading along the height of it, to the right and to the left, enfilading its defence, holding a wider and a wider gap, and the swords at either end of the line hacking and sweeping their way forward. And now (so many men having poured up the wall and along it) scraps of the many scaling ladders could be seen, and separate streams of men hurrying up them and reinforcing the lengthening line above that held the battlements. Until at last all the defence was brushed away, from east to west, and for a half-mile in one unbroken series the Crusaders were the masters of the rampart, and already men were hauling the scaling ladders over to descend into the city beyond. The men at the battering rams ran hard for the check-ropes, hanging desperately upon them to stop the swing, and the thuds ceased for the first time in all those hours. From the wooden tower also the attackers were scrambling down and racing towards the wall, and bringing new ladders and climbing it, now undefended. A lamentable confusion, masked by the screen of masonry, made up of scream and clamour, rose from the streets of the city within, as victory pressed on through the houses. Jerusalem had fallen; and already the first man in the race had thrust his palms against the walls of the Sepulchre, and sinking to his knees, collapsing, kissed it.

There is in the hills that shut in the garden of the Cotentin, in the depths of Normandy, a happy town with pastures and with orchards all around.

It is called the Silent Valley, Sourdeval. Here had a child been born in the castle of the place to the lord of it, and they had given him the name Robert, after the last great duke who was the leader of them all. This child Robert, grown a man, had armed himself and mounted himself, and followed the Crusade, and he it was who sprang first upon the wall of Jerusalem on that great day: Robert of Sourdeval, in the country of Avranches, under the shadow of the shrine which is called "St. Michael in peril of the sea." But even as he leapt upon the wall, and in the moment of his exaltation, he saw southward, upon the Tower of David, a great banner suddenly catching the sun, and he knew that it was the banner of Toulouse. From the south also the city had been forced, and he cried as he saw that banner, "Ville gagnée!"

*   *   *   *   *

Of the men who had followed and endured till the end and had entered Jerusalem, one from the Pyrenees, three years later, came home. A ship had taken him across the seas, pirates had captured it off Cyrene, and had shackled him as a galley slave; in the Balearics he had escaped by night with a Christian fisherman for guide.

They had made Narbonne, and so this man had come, darkened by the Eastern sun and lean and broken from the wars, home at last to his farm. There he found all those who had mourned him for dead, and his old father living still by the turf fire, but too forgetful of the world to welcome him. And as he told the old man of the wars, that old man only felt dimly in his fading mind (which was not wholly forgetful of Aragon and of Leon and the Cid Campeador) that all the world was full of fighting against Mahound.

Already five years past Huesca had been forced by Christian arms, and already three years past the Cid was dead.

THE LOSS OF AQUITAINE

(*March* 21, 1152)

EASTER came early in the year 1152, and that Lent was cold.

In the week before Palm Sunday, the middle week of March, the sodden roads of the great plains to the north and to the east of Orleans had trains upon them of men and wagons making all for Beaugency, two days below Orleans down the river—Beaugency, the little town at the opening of its shallow valley, standing upon the north bank of the Loire and facing the poor sun of this winter end.

There stood in the town of Beaugency, near the stream, a strong and simple castle, flanked with huge round towers. Many men have passed into possession of it, have rebuilt, and changed, and blazoned, and pulled down its stones in seven hundred years, but some of those towers still stand. It was, in this year 1152, Church land. It held of Amiens; and hither the Archbishop of Sens had summoned the Court and the king, Louis, and his queen, Eleanor, many lawyers and many barons, and the great prelates like

himself—of Rheims, of Rouen, of Bordeaux.
Their tenants for assessors, their squires and
hosts of serving men and troops of horse and
mules came crowding into the little place, turning
for a moment this half-forgotten town into a
capital; and the innkeepers were still dreaming of
gold, and every house was making itself a sort of
crowded hostelry; every barn was a stable.

The matter upon which this writ of the archbishop's had gone out to his king and the Court,
to the Queen Eleanor, and all their train, and to
his fellow bishops, and to the barons of France
and of Aquitane, was the great divorce. For
now that Louis, the king, had come back shamefully defeated from the Crusade (tortured by
rumours that were more than rumours of the
queen's contempt and unfaithfulness, heavily
warned that no son had been born of her to
continue the Capetian line), he was for ridding
himself of his burden. And this, although that
burden meant the mastery of half the south, and
rule direct from Paris over whatever lay between
the Pyrenees and the garden of the Loire; between the mountains of Auvergne and the sea.
For Eleanor had Aquitaine for her dower.

The king was a man of thirty. He was the heir
to that constant effort of the monarchy to turn

province by province from a proud fief into an immediate possession of the Crown. No wider sweep of that net had been thrown than when, in his boyhood, there had been brought to Rheims, as a wife for him, the girl who was heiress of all Aquitaine. He could also remember how, so many years before, that marriage had filled all his thoughts and all his heart in the new discovery of the south coming upon his cloistered mind. But life had turned sour.

*　　*　　*　　*　　*

The chapel of the castle, round-arched and broad, with very deep windows in its thick walls, and a faded fresco on its roof, was barely lit by the early light of the March morning. All were assembled for the great decision. Mass had been said. The ornaments of the place were veiled gloomily, as is the Lenten custom. The king's throne was set facing the bench where the bishops and their assessors sat; but the queen, with her women and her advocates, the tonsured clerks in her cause, and her barons of Aquitane, sat apart on the Gospel side of the nave, she also crowned and robed, she also expecting the release. Her tall figure, strong and too large in its rich draperies, suited her heavy, long face, over massive in the jaw, too steady and uncaring in the level of its high brow. Her kerchief fitted close, under the golden circle, to her now scanty hair.

The issue of this suit, which was predetermined, she strongly desired. She had said in her latest and angriest revolts: "I have married a monk and not a man!" And this, her thirtieth year, was for her also a culmination. She would bear the thing no more. For seven years she had had no child; when the children came they were daughters. She was not the mother of an heir. And the priests, by whom Louis VII. was himself so closely bound, offended her. She had hardly hidden her chance desires in the East, on the Crusade—a Greek, a noble, a Saracen slave. She had not hidden at all her contempt and her weariness. But there was more than that. She had now another choice.

Ten years, twelve years younger than herself, there was a lad into whose hands had tumbled, like ripe fruits from every side by converging inheritance, all the west: Brittany and Normandy and the Maine and Anjou from his father (for he was the Angevin), and from his mother England itself—for his claim to which crown he would fight and conquer, she knew. This lad, red-headed, passionately willed, and to be the master of such great domains, she had fixed down in her mind for a quarry. He would not fail her —for she would bring him Aquitaine. He should be lord over all the western seas from the hills of Cumberland right away to the Biscayans and Navarre. He was that young Henry of Anjou and Normandy, of Maine: and of England to be: a glorious young Lord, just past his nineteenth year. All these things the Queen Eleanor held in her heart that morning, masked behind her heavy, impassive face.

The loud, confused cries of hundreds talking in groups, of the lawyer-priests spreading their crackling parchments, and of serving men passing in and out of the doors, ceased to a sharp order from the archbishop's serjeant and the ringing of his pike upon the stone floor of that church. There were only a few hurried whispers passing between the clerks of the queen, and these also fell when the archbishop rose and gravely put his question, whether any one present desired to come forward on the plea of the king and of the queen that their marriage, being contracted within the decrees forbidden to Christian men and women, should be made null and of no effect. But if such consanguinity were not established, then let them preserve the sacrament of their marriage in God's name.

When he had sat him down again, those who stood ready behind the king—his relatives, and witnesses of his rolls and archives—came forward one after the other, and each stretched forward his right hand open, palm downwards, over the relics, taking the oath assigned. Such and such was the degree of consanguinity between Eleanor of Aquitaine and Louis VII, of that name, King of the French and Duke of Aquitaine. Eleanor, upon her throne apart, heard in those proud royal formulæ titles hardly greater than her own. She had behind her generation after generation of the great dukes, her fathers, of whom she came, the sole heiress, summing up in her presence the story of the Roman south, and Poitiers on its hill, and Bordeaux and Bayonne, and the vineyards of Angoulême. She would take good care into whose hands all those hundred miles of countryside should go. She foresaw the wars.

When the long and formal business of that Court was over (the depositions inscribed, signed and sealed, the pleas of either party heard, the documents declared, the relationship established), the bishops consulted for their verdict, and gave it in corporate form, so that the great clerics outside their body—the Pope, their chief, and even great St. Bernard himself (the spiritual master in Christendom)—said nothing more. They gave their verdict upon the undoubted text of the Canon Law. They declared this marriage of fifteen years now null. And their solemn sentence was delivered, the silence broke again for a moment, and once again the serjeant of the archbishop, with the pound of his pike upon the stone floor, commanded silence. The queen took from her head the gold circle of the woman's crown and set it down in symbol of the change. She had another crown before her eyes, and one that should be greater in Europe for fifty brilliant years than the crown of the Capetian. She was to be mistress of the Angevin, and to command in her own fashion, through so many wars, so great a government.

She was free now. She rose, not waiting to see whether the king should rise first from his throne apart. She withdrew with all her train, standing high at the head of those high lords, and moving towards the eastern doors. She went southward, and away to her own land.

These things were done before Easter, the

cold and leafless Easter of that year. The spring broke, and by Pentecost this woman had married the Angevin: young Henry of Anjou, of Maine, of Normandy, of England to be. And his honour also she broke at last.

THE PILGRIMAGE

LOUIS, King of France, the seventh of that
name, had no son. Two wives had borne
him four daughters. Their alliance confirmed
his house, but the Capetian foundation was im-
periled. It had established itself by an unshaken
chain of circumstance and will, son succeeding
father, and crowned in youth before the father's
eyes. It had been a process of power hidden in
the mind, a thing gradually more and more conscious for two hundred years, since first Robert
the Strong had come, no one knew whence, into
the Court, and obtained his government in the
west; since Hugh had been crowned. It was
now grown to full stature, and knew itself: a
thing formed—the kingship of France; and from
that seed, now a tree, was to grow the full kingdom and the re-establishment of the Gauls. But
now the advance was halted, for Louis, already
in middle age, had no son. Four years had passed
since his last marriage.

He was a pious man, full of doubt and intui-
tion. He prayed secretly to God, and there is

record of his prayer, "I beseech Thee, O God
. . ." For the great times that were to come
depended upon its answer. He prayed secretly
to God for a son.

When the time of the queen's delivery drew
near, the king summoned Hugh, the bishop, and
said to him, "Tell no one till I am dead, but I
have dreamed a dream which some survivor
should know. I have dreamed that what shall
soon be born stood holding a golden cup full of
blood, and that the nobles of France came around
and drank of it in turn."

In the night of the 21st of August, the vigil of
the Octave of the Assumption in the year 1165
from the Incarnation of the Lord, the child was
born in a castle to the south. It was a boy, and
they gave him the name of Philip, but for the
populace a second name, "Adeodatus," the gift of
God—so necessary was he to the Crown, and so
strangely had he come in answer to a prayer.
Later he was to be the Augustus, to fight great
and glorious battles all his life, to break the
Angevin and the German, and to rule all up to the
coasts of the sea.

Then for years the king watched over the child,
and cherished him as he grew: not so strong in

body as he should have been. All turned upon his life.

When the lad was already in his fourteenth year, the king summoned a great council in the spring time and said to the great lords and bishops there assembled, "I will, if it is your will, that my son be crowned at Rheims, and allegiance sworn to him by all while yet his father lives, as is the custom of our House, and this on the Assumption of this very year." This was the year 1179. For he felt his age coming upon him, though he was but in his sixtieth year. Already had he feared paralysis, and known the symptoms of its coming. His council acclaimed him and his will.

As the Feast of the Assumption drew near, which is also the memory of Roncesvalles, the 15th of August, Louis, the king, came with all his Court to the castle of Compiègne, on the edge of the great woods, there to stay till they should set out on the two days' march to Rheims, and the young prince, Philip, was with him.

But just in the days before this journey was due, the prince went out one morning with his men to hunt the boar in the forest at the gates of the castle. They gave him a swift horse, perhaps too mettlesome, and he rode out with his men in the morning, with their hounds and their horns, till, in the depths of this high wood, they unleashed, and next found a great boar; and him they pursued, scattering round, by this narrow path and that, through the thick undergrowth, and making round by the right and the left to come up with the hounds at last when they should pull the great boar down. But as his horse went furiously, and got off too far from the rest, the prince heard the horns more faintly, and, when he tried to rally to them, took false turnings, till at last he heard them no more. Then he knew that he was lost. He had not eaten, and the day was done, and he became afraid. Before it was dark he checked his tired mount and stood in doubt, looking all around and seeing nothing in the woods nor hearing any sound of men. Then he prayed to Our Lady and his Lord St. Denis, who is the strong protector of the Kings of France, that he might be saved out of the high wood; and looking round again to his right, he saw in the gloaming a charcoal burner, rough and forbidding, all grimy with his trade, and bearing on his shoulder an axe.

The child was frightened at that figure; but he took it for a sign, and summoning his courage he walked his horse up to the charcoal burner and accosted him very courteously, and told him that he was the Son of France lost in the high wood, and in peril, and weak with long fasting. This story the man believed, and he led the prince by ways he knew all through the miles of forest in the darkness, till, by morning, they had come to the castle of Compiègne, and the prince was delivered safe to his father. But the strain had thrown the boy into a fever, and it seemed he would die. Thus for the second time was the line of France in peril, and King Louis near despair.

In such an agony he bethought him of the saints, and what help he could implore. There was one with whose name all Christendom was alive—St. Thomas, murdered at Canterbury not ten years before by the agents of the Angevin, his rival. The archbishop had been his guest, he had succoured him—through policy and as a lever against the house which was his greatest feudatory, and almost his master; the house of Anjou, against which he had warred in vain. There, in England, its head, Henry, was a great king, his equal. Louis, the king, determined to pray at that shrine. They could not dissuade him. They told him it was perilous to put himself unarmed into his enemy's hand; they warned him of his failing powers, but his intention stood; and immediately after the Assumption he set out for the sea. His weakness hampered him. He was six days on his journey to the coast. He reached it at Wissant, on the Straits, in the evening of his son's fourteenth birthday, the 21st of August. On the morrow, the Octave of the Feast, he crossed the Narrows and came into Dover Harbour, an inlet of the hills, and so went ashore, the first King of France to land in this island. Henry, the king, came down to meet him, and they went together up to Canterbury to pray at the shrine. There, in the crypt, at the tomb under the high altar, King Louis prayed for his son's recovery and for the strength of the Capetian line.

King Louis had upon his finger a certain stone, the most precious and (some said) the greatest in the world; it was called the Royal Jewel, and men knew of it everywhere. All manner of stories were told of it: how it shone in the dark with a smouldering light, how it was worth the ransom of a kingdom, how the saint had claimed it in a vision. But these stories were only tales. The great stone was its own title. This stone King Louis took off as he knelt at the shrine, and offered it to be the saint's for ever. There they hung it, and later they put a silver angel before it, pointing to it. There the stone shone before the shrine three hundred years and more, displayed whenever the rich cover of the shrine was lifted for the pilgrims, and giving birth to legend upon legend; until, when more than three hundred years had passed, another King of Eng-lan—another Henry, the Tudor—destroyed that shrine. He, in his turn, took that famous stone and had it set in a ring to wear on his enormous thumb; and after him his daughter Mary had it set in a collar she wore; but what became of it after that, or where it is now, I do not know.

So the king gave the stone, and prayed at the shrine of St. Thomas for his son, who lay between life and death far off in France, the last of such a line.

Louis, the king, also gave to the monastery of Canterbury sixteen hundred gallons of wine a year for ever, to be taken from the product of his own vineyards at Poissy; a poor, thin, northern wine, but he could give no other, for as yet the southern vineyards were not in any domain of the Crown. And having done these things, and given great alms, his pilgrimage was ended, and on the third day, which was the 25th of August, he set forth back again to the sea coast at Dover, and on the morrow, the 26th, he crossed, reaching the French land.

His task was done. In his journey south to his own the blow fell on him. As he reached Paris all his right side was struck, and he was paralysed. The boy, however, his son, was saved.

On the day of All Saints, Prince Philip was crowned at Rheims with great splendour, in the midst of the twelve peers, and so was the full purpose of his father accomplished. But that father, in his illness, could not see the crowning, and in a little while he died, as well and piously as he had lived.

THE TRIUMPH OF SALADIN

(Battle of Hattin, Saturday, July 4, 1187)

THERE is a plain full of grass and reedy at the edges. It is sunk deep between high, bare limestone hills. It goes level with the southern edges of that clear lake which is called the Sea of Galilee.

Through this grassy plain to-day the railway to Damascus runs, and through that plain from the earliest of human years the ancient road from Damascus has come falling down from the great dark shelves of the Huran Mountains, standing in a wall thousands of feet high, eastward above the hot gorge of Jordan; beyond there is the desert land.

On the sward of this place lay encamped, with their tents, seven thousand of the Saracen cavalry, a chosen body to whom the Christians, still holding Palestine, would have given the name of "knights" or "nobles." Their leader (or rather their head, through the favour of his father) was a boy, el-Afdal, some seventeen years old, the son of Saladin.

For Saladin it was who thus lay in wait to

destroy our Christian hold upon the Holy Places of Our Lord.

It was the very end of April, when the spring of that land is turning into summer, and already the corn on the fields of the swelling heights to the west, the corn of the bare uplands of Galilee, was ripening. The year was the year 583 of the Hegira, when Mahomet's mission began—the eleven hundred and eighty-seventh from the Incarnation of our Lord, from which we Christians reckon.

The presence of this camp was singular.

There had never been—save in the crisis of the Crusades—a single issue of Moslem against Christian, of the French tongue against the Arabic, of Europe against Asia. Such issues only show clear in moments of intensity. But the great French feudatories, who between them held the Syrian coast and Palestine, those who had been Lords of the Levant since the First Crusade, three generations before, a small group, immensely rich, touched already (those who were not recently immigrant) by the Orient, inextricably related by marriage and re-marriage—these had between them feuds, alliances, dissolving groups of affection or ambition which made compromise possible with the enemy. So had their opponents over against them (the emirs of great towns, the sheikhs of tribes, the occasional armed leaders of new hordes) their own ambitions, local aims and reasons. These also had their perpetual intrigue. These also had been touched by the West as had the westerners by the East. In the cross-currents of all that swirl, you would find at moments a group of Frenchmen and Arab against a group of Arab and Frenchmen, Christian and Moslem against Moslem and Christian; so it had also been for now four hundred years on the Marches of Spain, two thousand miles away, on the other front of the great fight. There also the Cid Campeador had parleyed with the Moslem lords. The great current of our pouring out against Asia had such eddies on its banks.

On this side Jordan, over against the Saracen camp of cavalry (with its white tents marking the as yet unburnt sward), the land that rose hundreds of feet up to the other limestone hills of the west, the land of Galilee, had for master a man conspicuous among all the Europeans of his time.

He was a Capetian, of the French blood royal through the women; through his father he held directly from the first Crusading advance and conquest nearly a century before. His title he held from Tripoli, of which he was the Count. And this square of land between the lake and the sea was his, through his marriage with a woman who had brought it to him as her dower, and who reigned in what was also his capital and chief castle of Tiberias: the old town of Herod, between the inland water and the first spring of the hills. Now this man, at that moment, chief Christian though he was, consented to be, for policy, a man that still parleyed with Saladin, the new and tremendous leader of all that intended the end of the Christian name.

Raymond of Tripoli had reckoned himself of right, by the statute of his kinsman (the last adult King of Jerusalem), to be regent of the whole realm. It was his, not only in his own eyes, but in those of his peers, to administer from Jerusalem all the feudality of the Levant. It had been denied him, and denied him abruptly and recently, by a trick which had put a man incompetent for such office, a chance husband of the dead king's daughter, upon the throne. Guy of Lusignan, an uncertain man of whom posterity has thought perhaps less than it should, but whom certainly contemporary men despised; florid, perhaps unsoldierly, certainly of a sort which cannot make itself obeyed, he had come, through the intrigue of a court and the will of a very young woman, to be crowned; after her child, the true heir to the throne, had (perhaps mysteriously) died. The Master of the Templars, a man French in speech but from Bideford in Devon, a brave but hasty man, had helped in this, and the degraded Patriarch of Jerusalem, half Oriental, sunk in a harem, had concurred—why we do not know.

The Count of Tripoli, Raymond, in great anger had gone off northward disappointed of the crown, and most of the barons were with him in the quarrel.

The secession was, in a manner, self-defence. Count Raymond called it to himself the restoration of order; legitimacy; the first step to a strong state. But what he did was to make some understanding with Saladin, which popular tradition and the poets (with their sense for the heart of things) have handed all down the centuries for treason.

It was not as though Raymond had made up one of those ephemeral compacts of local truce with the small and changing leaders of the desert which men would soon forget. The compact— or whatever it was—was with Saladin. The shadow of Saladin had increased enormously, rapidly, like the shadow of a great tree at evening, and in such few years that they seemed (to a man then full grown) like so many days.

That son of Job, Saladin, the Kurd from the Tigris, had swallowed up his masters, one after the other, by intrigue, by violence, by that sort of fatality which drives the conquerors, and which has in it so intimate a mixture of enthusiasm, hypocrisy, and terrene desire.

The whole business had not covered more than the life of that young son, el-Afdal, seventeen years old, who lay there encamped beyond Jordan. When Afdal was a new-born child, Saladin was still a servant. To-day he was imperial. It was a space of time no longer than the space between the last two wars of the English (that in South Africa and the Great War). In that little time Saladin had come to be master of the whole vast Syrian and Mesopotamian and Desert and Egyptian spaces which encircled the Christian bastion of the Holy Land.

Saladin was as much a master at Cairo as at Damascus. He was obeyed from the Gulf of Aleppo to the Persian hills; from the Armenian boundaries to the Soudan. This immense power was in the hands of a man whose varied purpose certainly included a fixed desire to trample down the Christian name, not only to the sea, but (if that were possible) beyond the sea. Our little European outpost of The Sepulchre, stronger in blood and faith and tenacity by far than anything around it, had always for a century been abominably outnumbered. Now for the first time in a century it found those numbers all organized under one man, and that man certainly a great soldier, and everywhere also obeyed and everywhere victorious. He was about them to the north, to the east, to the south. He was gathering his armies. The hum of the swarm was heard all over the East.

His parleying with such a force and such a threat—no matter with what excuse of statecraft—could not be forgiven Raymond of Tripoli. He called his diplomacy many names to himself. He called it this, that, and the other. He thought it necessary, perhaps, as an expedient to the Christian society, which was so threatened. He argued, perhaps, for delay. He certainly was moved—though he might have denied it—by wounded pride. He none the less played a part, as he thought, for Christendom. But he and it were to pay a terrible price for so much intelligence and so little vision.

This white camp of Saracen cavalry, on the

sward to the south of the lake, was the match
that lit the explosion.

We know what proceeded from it; what we
cannot to-day explain is the motive, either upon
the one side or upon the other, which led to the
fantastic tourney: it was in part a jest or stage
play, in part a challenge. It is of a time other
than ours—we can only half understand. There
are but a few words remaining to guide us.

At any rate there proceeded from el-Afdal and
his seven thousand a request (not a demand) that
the Saracen horsemen should ride westward into
Galilee, through Galilee, and return. That they
should pass one day in so riding courteously
round through the territory of Galilee.

Raymond of Tripoli returned them a sort of
set licence, marked out curiously like the rules
of a game: "That they should not mount until
the sun had risen, and that they should promise
to be back over Jordan before it had set. That
they should do no damage or injury; that they
should kill none, nor burn nor pillage."

What caused the request? Why were these
terms accepted and observed? We cannot tell.
The request was made, and in that form granted
and accepted. Whether it was an outward symbol of the truce with Saladin through this favour

to his son, or a permission to ride out and seek forage, by agreement; for whatever reason, the request was made and granted as I have said; and the 1st of May, 1187, was fixed for so singular an adventure. It was the Feast of St. Philip and St. James.

The Count Raymond sent round throughout his wife's land of Galilee that on this coming day of the Saracens' Ride no man should appear in the fields, lest by accident there should be provocation. He feared lest, after that hushed, expectant, toppling mood, which the enormous preparations of Saladin had now imposed upon all the East, there should suddenly be heard the roar of an explosion. All his subjects were to be within their farms, or behind the walls of their towns; all cattle were to be driven within their byres and folds. The seven thousand infidel lances were to ride round through an empty land, and so return.

They set out northward after they had crossed Jordan, followed the bank of the lake, challenged, as they passed, the gates of Tiberias; but, true to their compact, they shot no arrow, they threw no javelin. They rode on up to Nazareth, where it slopes to the south on the Galilean hills— Nazareth the chief point of their hatred. They passed under the walls of the little town with insults, but with no act of arms. They rode yet farther, fatiguing their light mounts, until they could look down the hills across the great plain of Esdraelon to the height of Carmel, and even to a glimpse of the sea. They had ridden more than twenty miles deep into Galilee before the leaders turned rein to reach their camp again down in the deep trench of Jordan, to cross the river and to find their tents.

It was already late in the afternoon, but the sun still high in the sky (and their terms therefore strictly kept) when, as they halted their tired beasts near the lake shore under the hills before the crossing of the river, they saw a strange sight.

Less than one hundred mounted men, heavily armoured as was the fashion of the Franks, sitting their larger horses, already deployed as though for battle, came over the last crest and began slowly moving down the slope above them.

They watched the sight curiously. If this unknown band intended battle, it was challenging odds of nearly a hundred to one. But why had they appeared?

The brilliant summer day had been marked throughout by the silence of all that countryside;

by the absence not only of soldiery, but even of peasants and their kine. This little line of isolated knights, with nothing in support and no one near, might have seemed a mirage for its futility. But it was real enough against the falling hillside under the westering sun. Since so small, novel, unexpected a force seemed to propose a challenge before the Moslem cavalry could cross the Jordan, that large Saracen force deployed in turn on its small tired horses, and awaited the charge. They took their favourite formation of a shallow crescent—the universal tactic of their time against the weight of a European charge. They drew back the centre from the main blow, and trusted by numbers to develop in the wings. So stood the hundredfold cavalry of the Mahommedans, expecting the shock and their own inevitable victory.

Why had this small Christian force so appeared?

This is what had happened.

The King of Jerusalem had sent two great messengers to Count Raymond of Tripoli. He desired, if it might be, to compose his quarrel. He felt the coming of the storm.

These two messengers were the heads of the

great military orders—the Master of the Knights Templar and the Master of the Hospital.

They had come so far upon their journey northward as Nazareth, and lay there upon the night before Afdal's ride. There, at Nazareth, they had received the message which Raymond had sent round the whole countryside, warning them against provoking Afdal, when that son of Saladin should come outside the walls. Of these two men, one merits a particular attention: the Master of the Temple. I have just written of him.

He was a knight, French in speech, Gerard by name, doubtless from Bideford, in Devon. A man of energy and even of violence, of ambition in government, of great courage, too personal in hatred, and alive with the splendid traditions of his Order in arms. He it was who had most supported the young queen in Jerusalem, most helped to make her husband the king, most thwarted the high claims of the Count of Tripoli. All this must be remembered to understand what follows.

This man, Gerard, then, the Master of the Templars, was there in Nazareth that afternoon of the 30th of April, upon the eve of Afdal's ride. And when he heard Count Raymond's order, he took it—quite wrongly—for treason.

This is the note of the tragedy that was to come two months later. *This* is the evil thread running through all the story of our disaster in the East— the legend of Raymond's treason had taken root.

Raymond of Tripoli had preferred the political way to the direct. He had parleyed with Saladin. And on that account he, by far the greatest soldier of them all, lost direction, and, in spite of his genius, saw Jerusalem and all Palestine go down.

Later he died of the shame.

The two Masters, I say, he of the Temple and he of the Hospital, had received Raymond's order—to keep quiet within walls. This is the way they treated it. They sent at once to such knights of their two societies as were within riding distance of the town. They gathered less than one hundred. They harangued them in the market-place of Nazareth, saying it was foul shame to stand unmounted and with the sword sheathed while the Saracens rode unchallenged through the open country, with their high minaret cries of insult and defiance. The little group of knights was moved; for the whole spirit of their foundation was to risk odds and to sacrifice themselves perpetually. They cared nothing for numbers. With their footmen to serve them, perhaps four hundred (and these seem to have straggled and to have been left behind), they rode out before evening from the northern gate of Nazareth, and so eastwards, following the retirement of Afdal. Hence it was that Saladin's son had seen them, as I have described, suddenly appearing upon the fall of the hill above them, a handful of armed men upon their larger horses, confronting a force more than a hundred times their own.

The Templars and the Hospitallers charged. They were surrounded; nearly all fell; but in the course of the *mêlée* the execution they did was so great that the day remained legendary with the enemy. One especially, James (who came from Maille, in Touraine, and who was among the last survivors), they thought (did the Saracens) to be St. George himself upon a white horse; for in both armies there was this superstition or vision as old as the battle of Konieh, that St. George was to be seen leading the Christian ranks. His enemies stood round the dead man with lifted hands, the dread of unseen things upon them. They wiped the sweat and blood and dust from his face, and carried him off like a relic, still thinking him something from beyond this world.

When the slaughter was done, and all save,

perhaps, some five or six of that little band had fallen (some cut their way out, we know, for we find them in the later battle), Afdal stuck Christian heads on his lances in triumph and rode on, and, with his reduced thousands, crossed Jordan just before the setting of the sun; and such was the end of that day's foray.

When the news of it came to Tiberias to Count Raymond, he saw at once the enormity of the moment. In numbers insignificant, their action should be forgiven as heroic; but the separate policy, the contempt for his orders, the provocation offered by these few knights, would surely set in movement that great machine, the rumbling of whose wheels all the East was expecting. It was a challenge to Saladin, the very challenge which Saladin thirsted for: and Raymond sweated to delay catastrophe. The challenge had been given prematurely in spite of him, and to the ruin of his plans. It could not now be undone.

Raymond of Tripoli forgot, in the common cause, the past and its angers. He hurried south to Jerusalem. He was reconciled to Guy of Lusignan. All the Christian knights became one body. The bravest and most spirited of them all, the high-born adventurer Reginald, who held the strong outpost, Kerak, on the south of the Dead

Sea; who had, in raid after raid, harassed the rich caravans of the desert; who, with an amazing energy, had approached, in the height of summer, the Red Sea itself (sending his ships in sections over the desert on camels), and menaced the holy places of the enemy hundreds of miles away—Reginald, whom Saladin hated with a personal hatred for his fearlessness and his unbroken power, at whose castle only that winter he had impotently shaken his spear: Reginald of Chatillon came riding in. The garrisons were withdrawn from the towers of the sea-coast and from the towns—from Askalon, from Gaza, from Acre, from Tyre. Two thousand knights and barons, fully armed, were gathered together, and such a full levy meant, with all their sergeants and their footmen, a force of fifty thousand. They were more; for the Eurasians, called "Turcopoles," went with them lightly mounted—of no great service save, perhaps, to observe.

A meeting-place was discussed. It was chosen, I think, by the advice of Raymond (for once accepted by his peers), at a point over against the only road whereby the host of Saladin could come—that is, in the very heart of Galilee.

For Saladin, based on Damascus, must strike just to the north or just to the south of the Lake of Tiberias, and almost certainly by the main road south of it—the road that has seen unnumbered armies pass since the beginning of human life upon those hills.

In the choice of this gathering-place, right in the heart of Galilee, you have one of those curious marriages between the symbolic and the real of which history is full. The place chosen (because even in the height of summer it had ample water) was that of the village, the plain, the wells of Sepphoris: which they call to-day "Seffurieh."

What an arena for the great issue between the rival forces of the world! Not four miles south over the hill was Nazareth; not four miles east was Cana of Galilee. A day's march beyond Nazareth, over the valley which Nazareth commands, was Nain. The tradition of the Transfiguration looked at them from Mount Tabor, and the plains below had seen Saul creep by night to find the dead at Endor, and had watched the rush of Barak from the mountain slopes against the heathen, and had heard the song of Deborah. Far below them, in the flat, ran the Kishon. A day's walk to the east was the town of the Magdalen, and the shores of that little inland sea round which is set half the story of the Gospels.

Here to the Wells of Sepphoris they came,

then, from all the points of the Holy Land, riding in; and that great fragment of the True Cross, the standard of the Crusades, was sent to be the heart of the host in this last trial.

So they gathered.

Meanwhile the mighty instrument which threatened them was gathering too. Saladin, who had earlier been south in the desert, in the dark hills beyond the Dead Sea, had come back north. He had summoned all his troops from as far as the Tigris, and the Orontes, and the borders of Egypt. Twelve thousand of the knights alone—that is, of men who held rank by what the Christians would have called "noble tenure"—were in his muster; with, perhaps, six or seven or ten times as many—an unknown multitude—of lesser soldiers eager for "Allah's road"; the holy business of uprooting the Nazarenes: that is, ourselves; Europe; Christendom.

Saladin also had his gathering-place—Ashtaroth, on the great pilgrims' road in the Hauran, two days' march east of Jordan, four days' from Damascus. Thence going a few miles northward (much to where the station of Tesil now stands on the Damascus railway) he reviewed that vast host of varied men.

It was a Friday, the holy day of the Moslem

week, on which day the great fanatic loved to begin an enterprise—Friday, the 26th of June, 1187, the fourteenth day of the month of Rabi-el-Aker, in the five hundred and eighty-third year of the Hegira. On that same day, at the hour of public prayer, he began his march, and, going far, encamped his army that night where his son's cavalry had stood two months before in the plain to the east of Jordan, just south of the Sea of Galilee.

There for a space he halted. His scouts and spies went cautiously westward over the burnt fields and stubble of the blazing summer for news, and brought back the numbers and names of this gathering of the Christian host at the Wells of Sepphoris.

Saladin took counsel with his captains, and it was determined to provoke immediate action, for the superiority of the Moslems was very great.

Upon Monday, the 29th, the host crossed Jordan and entered Galilee, camping immediately upon the hither bank, and making no true march that day. But upon the 30th they advanced westward some seven miles on to the higher land, and stood at Kefr Sabt, astride the direct way between Nazareth and Tiberias, ten miles or so to the east of the Christian camp at Sepphoris.

The Christian host did not move.

Saladin, by one of those actions in which a soldier compels or provokes something military through something political, detached a force to ruin Tiberias. It was Raymond's capital of Galilee, and there in the stronghold were Raymond's wife and her children. Hoping that such a provocation would compel a decision, the Sultan, leaving a considerable force at Kefr Sabt, moved the mass of his troops somewhat northward to cover with their camp the main road between Sepphoris and Tiberias; while the third body, dispatched against Tiberias itself, did their work. This second camp of his in Galilee lay on the broad plateau south of a little village called HATTIN. This plateau was the watershed between the gullies (dry at such a season) which run down to the Mediterranean and the streams and fountains fully supplied which take their short course eastward by a fall of many hundred feet into the trench of the Jordan valley and the Sea of Galilee. From Tiberias itself, and the shores of the lake, Saladin's camp stood but half an hour's ride away, and meanwhile the force he had detached (and led) to reduce Tiberias was burning the town.

Raymond's own wife was close besieged upon

the rocky acropolis of it, threatened every moment with disaster. She sent, as Saladin had hoped she would send, entreaties to the Christian host that they would march east at once and succour her and her garrison. It was she (the daughter of the Lord of St. Omer) who had brought Galilee to Raymond for her dower. Her four children were with her, and death was upon them all.

It was upon Thursday, the 2nd of July, that her passionate letter came in to the Christian camp, at vespers, in the late afternoon of the day. In the great red tent of Guy, the King of Jerusalem, the council was held.

It seemed a clear task to march at once to the relief of the capital; a first day's march and a battle upon the second should decide the issue—and surely time pressed most urgently.

Then it was that Raymond himself rose in the crowded assembly, under the red light that glared through the hangings of the pavilion, and made a speech which all but changed the story of the world.

Those who had heard of him only by name crowded around Raymond to see so famous a figure. What did they see?

A little, very thin man, scanty of hair, and

that hair very flat upon his head. He was dark, abstemious, spare, with brilliant, piercing eyes; older than the run of those knights; a light weight on horseback; hardly (to look at) a strong swordsman, but with the just reputation of soldiership beyond any other man there. His French words rose.

The moment he began to speak it was seen that his advice would run counter to the universal counsel of those lords.

"I shall surprise you," he said. "I shall prefer the interests of the State to my own. My own country is overrun. It is my people who are suffering death and slavery; my town that is in flames; my wife who is besieged and crying for succour. Everything draws me to relieve Tiberias, except my business as a Christian, which is to serve the common cause at the cost of my own disaster."

He bade them not attack but stand fast where they were, supplied with ample water. Between them and Saladin's position, south of Hattin, in this brazen height of the summer, not a drop would be found in the baked gullies. The infidel army covered all the springs and the lake behind them. It was but ten miles, but those ten miles would spell disaster. Let Tiberias go. The Sultan would be compelled to attack very soon. *His* then would be the fatigue, *his* the thirst. And his retirement, should he be checked, would be through a hostile country. We even find, in the record of what is told of his speech, some hint of stratagem. It may be that Raymond, with his clear eye for war, had ready some force for watching the passages of the Jordan, and threatening to cut off Saladin's retirement.

So he spoke, as the evening lengthened, after the time of vespers, upon that Thursday, the 2nd of July. No one believed him. Though none said it in his presence, he felt it in the air around him that he was already, in their legend, the traitor. Whatever he advised, their minds conceived as the trick of something too astute for a loyal man-at-arms. And when his advice had been given there was a murmur and a rumour all round.

But as discussion followed and broadened, the older or more poised men weighed fully what the Count of Tripoli had said. For a time, as night approached, their argument was gaining, and the council was perhaps dispersing (or had dispersed) with the determination to stand fast and await the attack of Saladin. But after darkness had fallen, whether in full council or alone, that man who thought himself the counterpoise to Raymond, and who thoroughly believed in Raymond's treason, Gerard of Bideford, came to King Guy and urged and urged the folly of listening to any plan coming from a man who, to the public shame, had once bargained with Saladin.

The king, Guy of Lusignan, changed again, and perhaps his council with him. At any rate, he was obeyed, Raymond's advice neglected; and at dawn the great host began its fatal march and fighting of Friday, the 3rd of July, 1187.

At the head of the column rode Raymond himself and his immediate vassals, the men of Galilee, and those from Tyre and the north, as though to prove at once his discipline in what he now thought a lost cause and his readiness to take the sacrifice. After, with the main body trailing along the road of that upland, through the parched fields, came King Guy himself and the guard round the fragment of the True Cross; while the Knights Templar under their passionate Devonshire leader, in part the cause of so much evil, and their brethren, the Hospitallers, covered the train and baggage at the rear.

The sun rose, the heat immediately struck, and with it struck also here and there, harassing the flanks of the column, forbidding the army elbow room, appearing and disappearing through the thick dust, the hornets of Saladin. Those light horsemen darted, skirmishing on their rapid desert mounts, armed with the long light lance, and pricking, as it were, and goading the cumbersome body, whose surface alone as yet they could irritate, and which yet they could so gravely impede.

The sun still rose; the heat increased; men straggled; there were too frequent delays and uncommanded halts; blocks in the column. And all the while the Saracen swarm grew and grew on either side, almost encircling. Still the long column struggled forward. Before noon began the complaint for water. Of all the gullies crossed in the first slow dusty seven miles or so, not one had so much as a stagnant pool between its hot stones. Such gourds as men had with them were long ago consumed, and of other provisions of water for such a host there was none, and could be none in those days.

They had passed by Cana of Galilee, they had come to the bare upland plateau, where the air danced in the heat over the glaring limestone, and the broad rough track of the earthen road was a fog of scorching dust. It was the early afternoon. The still increasing masses of enemy horse striking and turning again, shepherding in their enemy, almost surrounded the Christians. Already some grave disorder was appearing in that three miles or more of exhausted men. In a halt deliberately called Raymond once more gave his last advice—once more to be wasted. He told King Guy that there could be nothing ahead but disaster for a force which had fallen so suddenly into such a condition—a condition inevitable in attempting such a march through such a country at such a season, and with such forces against such a foe. Moreover, they were threatened with envelopment. One way out remained, and only one. It was to wheel round to the right—that is, south-eastward; to cut their way through to water that night in the valley of the Fejjas brook, and with the morning, refreshed, to hold the passages of the Jordan. Then let Saladin, if he will, come down south against them. Short of breaking their defence, his retreat was cut off, and his great host was ruined. Again Guy of Lusignan hesitated. Perhaps Raymond's plan would have won; but in the midst of this deliberation, the harassing Mahommedan cavalry took on another aspect, more severe than the last. They came on in full force. They rode round the host. They not only cut into the flanks but into the

Knights Templar with their baggage to the rear, and the end of that day of torture and thirst was spent up to nightfall in a full battle against a perfect circle of foes. Many of the stragglers had already fallen out in each episode of confusion, and had passed to death or slavery. The now depleted, fainting column camped that night; still an organized body, but terribly shaken and already doomed. It was a night of agony and of alarm. Long before morning that army of the Cross and Europe was already defeated.

All through the short darkness men implored and fought for water, and could not obtain it. Upon so much agony worse came. The Saracens set fire to the dry bushes of that limestone upland, and under a light wind the smoke drove through the Christian camp. Raymond, in the van, knew that the dice had fallen. "He called upon God the Lord, and said that the realm was ruined." It was so.

The dawn of the Saturday broke. Raymond, with the van, took horse, and saw before him, dark against the sunrise, the strange twin saddle peaks which they call the Horns of Hattin, the watch towers of that land. At their foot stood deployed the main body of Saladin; the rest of his followers were on either side. The envelopment was complete. There, behind the Saracens, was water, food. The enemy fought refreshed against ghosts of men.

Their armament was stronger too. All the Saracen munitionment was carefully distributed for a certain victory. The camels, with their loads of arrows, were ranged behind the archers, and there was a great reserve as well. It is true that, had the Christian army been by some miracle in condition for strong action, the Sultan's position was very perilous. He was right on the lake, with very steep falling land only a few hundred yards behind him, and his only road of retreat passed just behind the fronts of the two armies. If those fronts shifted in his disfavour, if his light men broke at the shock of the heavier Franks, that road would be cut. Whether the unfavourable position weighed with him or no, whether he had fully gauged the breakdown of what was now before him, we cannot tell. He seems, up to the very end of the fight, to have had some doubt, tugging nervously at his beard and saying, "It was not yet over!" The historian, with both conditions before him, and knowing what exhaustion now weighed upon the Christians, can have none.

It was again, though on a much larger scale,

in that same formation of a shallow crescent, that the heart of the Moslem force—that in front of the head of the Christian host under Raymond—was drawn up. It did not at once attack, perhaps depending upon the sun and the heat as allies; and when it did so, it opened with a violent discharge of arrows. The effect of this was clinched by a general advance of the whole Mahommedan line at the charge. It caught and gripped the Christian body, separated its units, reduced the battle to a great mêlée, in which numbers, a better order, and—far more important than everything else—*condition,* were wholly upon the side of the enemy. There is no plan possible of this surging business, for no scheme was necessary or attempted. It was a cutting off of large isolated bodies, a cutting down of smaller ones, and a quantity of hand-to-hand fighting between men refreshed and men maddened by thirst; and for the most part the Christian infantry that followed the Christian knights was already in the mood for surrender, or even for accepting death.

Raymond, Count of Tripoli, with his knights, charged at the king's command right forward into the press. He found against him the Sultan's nephew, who opened his ranks and closed them after the small body of knights had crashed through. Raymond found himself with his companions cut off far forward. He hacked his way out through the mass of the Arab horses, and rode with his few companions straight for Tyre. There fell upon him a stupor, and later a frenzy, to see Christendom thus ruined. In a few weeks he was dead.

The footmen, the ill-trained levies from the towns, the half-armed peasantry, had already suffered massacre or surrendered in great groups of thousands. The struggle had not lasted the day long. It was perhaps hardly noon when one small remnant of the Christian host, crowding round the king, still held out. Of the fully armed men there were but one hundred and fifty: with their followers a few score more. The central point which they were guarding was the fragment of the Holy Cross, and what they were defending was a little mound on which there still stood the great red tent of the king. It fell, and the last of the fight was over.

That evening, in the tent of Saladin (which he caused to be pitched right in the heart of the battlefield), there took place an encounter of the two spirits of Europe and of Asia—of Western chivalry and of Oriental hate face to face.

This is what happened. The conqueror caused

to be seated upon his right the broken King of Jerusalem, half dead with the thirst and the heat of that day. Saladin gave him the first water he had tasted for many hours. There stood also before him Reginald of Chatillon, whom he had so hated with the violence of a religious hate for his audacity, his splendid courage, and, above all, for his threat to the holy cities of Islam. This man was now in his power, and the Sultan acted as Asia acts in such a pass. He abused him violently, reminded him of the unforgivable crime— that he had dared approach Mecca—dragged in the excuse of the raided caravans, and then fell upon the unarmed man himself to murder him, but not before he had heard the knight tell him that he would not save his life at the cost of faith, and answering with the pride of a man completely indifferent to death. This furious and horrible thing was not sufficient. Reginald of Chatillon, Lord of Kerak, was dragged out, still alive, and hacked to death by the guards. Then the conqueror gave orders that the most gallant and the strongest of his prisoners, those most symbolic of the faith which he hated—I mean the Knights of the Hospital and of the Temple—should be massacred. He knew that they always refused ransom. There were two hundred of these men.

They were butchered before the victorious army in a public place.

This was the end of the fight which decided the vast affair between our people and those of the East. Thenceforward, point by point, we lost the mastery of the Mediterranean; we admitted the stranger everywhere. We sowed that harvest of tragedy which is to-day the Balkans, the Dardanelles, the isolation of the Slav. Spain only we recovered. And as for the fragment of the Cross, they carried it away to Damascus. Jerusalem was theirs that autumn. Whose is it to-day?

CHÂTEAU GAILLARD

(*March* 6, 1204)

PHILIP AUGUSTUS, the King of France, sat upon a stone; it was a rough block of stone that lay, not yet used by the builders, on the rampart of his lines before Château Gaillard.

The huge building lay before him like a town —but such a town as no sight we see to-day can recall. Mass upon mass of sheer masonry— worked limestone—carefully jointed, and towering wall within and above wall, angle conflicting with angle in a hundred ways, and the whole an effort of shoulders and of rock. These things were (their ruins are) a sort of sacrament in human strength. What man can do to defend himself against man was there visible and tangible and amenable to common standards: apparent to a child as much as to a mathematician. And it was not only a sacrament of strength and of defence appalling in its dumb solidity and hugeness, but also a sacrament of labour, of energy manifest and achieved. It was also new and white.

Philip Augustus, the king, was an engineer. Every trace of the ditch, of the three circumvallations, of bastion and of angle, meant for him just what it should mean. He understood the co-relation of every part in that vast whole. It was for him what a score of music is to those rare men who can read and take pleasure in music from its mere printed signs though no instrument is sounding. And as he meditated the attack he admired. His creative soul was full of that creation which another such soul had ordered—Richard, the Angevin, the Lion Heart, now dead.

The King of France, thus sitting alone (for he would not be accompanied in such a meditation), watched the big thing with his chin upon his hand. He was a man in his fortieth year; his broad, square, somewhat flat face already definitely marked with the fixed passions of the mind and the habits of his long effort of recovery and of triumph. His eyes were a little cautious for those of a soldier, but very steady, and had in them that sort of secret smile which goes with the certitude of delayed achievement. His thin nose, and the slight sneer about his pressed lips, betrayed the same emotion as he pondered. His great head, rather bald for his age, was bare, and did not move in his contemplation of the mighty problem before him.

The foundations of the work were below him, as were its vast surrounding ditch and its first low containing wall. But the turrets and the battlements, with their wooden, jutting platforms, stood immensely above him, and higher still that enormous central keep which was the stake of the entire concern. It stood inhumanly large up against the keen March air, and the wind blew upon it from down the broad river valley and the distant sea. It had in it all the magnificence of Normandy. Down below, hundreds of feet, where the wide river ran, the Seine, he could see the burnt timber houses of Lesser Andelys, surrounded by its wall which he had stormed months before; the ruins also of the outworks upon the island by which he had approached across the stream. He heard, but did not see, the carts in perpetual rumble and the footmen tramping across his bridge of boats below. He heard the hammering of wood and the sawing of stone in his own lines, and in his mind he recalled, as he so sat, the long business of the siege.

Here was the test! This place, once fallen, he had forced the gate of Normandy, the last province which could defy his arms and his sovereignty. For now three hundred years and more it had been a kingdom almost apart from his own, though in feudal tenure responsible to him and to his house. John the Angevin, last Duke of Normandy, no longer the young man but still the great soldier, had abandoned the Normans—now five months ago. He was back in England. And here, before Philip, Roger of Lascy, with his superb little garrison, was still holding out, and until the castle fell there was no passing north into the Caux country or into the Calvados, no seizing of rich Caen or of Rouen, the mistress of all that land.

Philip, the king, remembered the long adventure. The advance up the wide valley of the Seine until, a march away, he first saw, whiter than the white scars of chalk on which it stood, the splendid new work of Richard gleaming far off like a challenge. He remembered the storming of the outworks on the island, the laborious fighting into Andelys, the rush of the refugees into the castle. He remembered the abominable winter, and his alignment of the strict blockade: the sentries calling to each other round the lines through the long, frozen nights. He remembered, not with pleasure, that awful day in which Roger of Lascy had turned out all the useless mouths, the refugees from the town below—the old men, and the children, and the women; their helpless panic, stumbling to and fro between the outer wall and his own lines; their hideous famine, and the blood, and at last his own clemency, and his permission that they should pass through and be fed.

Now the first breath of spring had come, and still the strict blockade was of no avail. Five months had gone, and nothing had been done save to contain that little band within, which still mounted guard surely in regular fashion, whose taunts could still be heard in the rough jibes shouted by night against his sentinels, and whose arrows, when they went down wind, sometimes just reached his lines, and had cost him men here and there. As he sat there he determined, for all great odds and risks, that an assault must be delivered even against so tremendous a body of resistance. Much lay in that decision; but Philip, the soldier, was a man who would arrive at a plan with increasing swiftness of judgment, and, having arrived at it, would as suddenly execute his desire.

There went through the lines the order for the attack, and the whole aspect of the camps surrounding the castle, one great oval linked by continuous works, was changed. The business was now no longer to starve but to destroy—and the murder of Arthur of Brittany should be avenged in violence.

*   *   *   *   *

First they made a great way, very broad and hardened everywhere with stone, along which the engines and the wooden towers could be hauled. Then, at night, they threw into the first outer main ditch earth and faggots from the woods on the hill above and all the refuse of the camp, and they began that week to struggle against the corner bastion of the outer wall. It was undermined in its foundations—the sappers' work defended by vigorous fire from the causeway against the battlements of the tower, and by the repeated shocks from the catapults and the rams, until, in some few days, the hard chalk rock having been tunnelled thoroughly, down came a whole segment of the outer wall, and the first circuit was in the hands of the king. Next, in the same fashion, was the second circuit attempted; and this, far less extended, concentrating its men more thoroughly, resisted with greater power. The engines did nothing against it. It seemed that the assault must fail.

Now there was in King Philip's army a soldier

called Bogis, an obscure man loving ruse, and he found that in certain wooden outworks of the place there was an entry to be made by those who could cunningly avoid the sentinels, and he, with a small band, went in there. But just as they thought to hold this entry, the besieged caught them, and, as being the quickest way to drive them out, set fire to this little building. It was a ruinous plan. Both had they—the besieged themselves—to retire from the fierceness of the flame, and also they were, by the effect of the fire when it was over and done, left with a gap in their defences, so that though the first intruders had been beaten back, Philip's men could pour through the charred breach.

They were at the third wall, the high wall round the donjon keep, and this was taken by mere strength and at vast loss and at storm. But of Lascy's very loyal band not two hundred remained, and all of them defending the wall, so that when they were cut off by the many thousands of Philip Augustus, the king, they could not post even a rearguard to defend the rush into the keep itself, though that was but a few yards behind; and so, upon the Saturday, the 6th of March, 1204, those that had not fallen in the fight were taken each separately between the wall and the tower. And the Saucy Castle, Richard the Lion Heart's eldest daughter, so young and so strong, had fallen.

* * * * *

It was the greatest feat of arms, almost, of the Middle Ages. It was to the French monarchy and the re-constitution of the land what Wattignies, six hundred years later, was to be for the defence and the survival of the Revolution. It was the opening of Normandy and the advent of all the host into the rich province of the north; the most stalwart, the most lengthily organized of all the feudal things that had proposed to withstand the re-integration of France. Through that breach in Château Gaillard's wall, as through a break in a dike, the flood of France poured through, armed, into the deep pasturage, the loaded wealth, the granaries, and the orchards of Normandy. And with Normandy so held under, that summer France was made again. And Philip Augustus, the king, became something almost more than a king as kings were accounted in that time. For he became a strict ruler over not one fief or two of his own, but over fief after fief that had formerly been bound only by plea and service, not in subjection, to his fathers. And it almost seemed as though Rome were returning.

This conqueror so conquering had about him, as he entered the Norman towns after his victory, a physical character of conquest, and there was a monk away in Tours, a canon of St. Martin's there, who saw him and knew him, and tells us well enough what he was:—

"A man high coloured, of a nature driven to good cheer, and to women and to wine, large to his friends, sparing to those who displeased him, an engineer, in faith Catholic, cautious for the future, stubborn in a resolution formed; he judged at once and directly. Fortune loved him, though he was too careful of his life. He was easily both roused and appeased. He loved to be served by the many and to think himself a tamer of the proud. Of the Church he was a good protector, and he nourished the poor."

THE CONVERSATION OF THE KING

(1245–1250)

ST. LOUIS, the king, loved quiet speech, meeting the speech of others. He loved rallying and conversed with all as though with peers. Pomp wearied him, even where it was necessary for the dignity of so great a state. Those jests which complete a question and leave no more to be said he was amused to hear. Also he himself observed men with very great wisdom, often silently; and his eyes, which were a little weary even in youth from too much questioning of himself and of the world, and from too much business of fighting of every kind within and without, were always luminous and often smiled. His body, which was spare, exercised by continual chivalry and by the weight of arms, but a little wasted by solicitude, by mortification, and by occasional disease, suited his gesture and the holy irony with which he salted life.

All those, or nearly all, who came about the king—men themselves, for the most part, much grosser in temper or much less subtle in observation—felt this play of his intelligence upon theirs, and when he was dead remembered it most vividly. Nor were the words of St. Louis and his manner things very conscious. They surrounded his personality like an air, impossible to define, easy to taste. They were a perfume. Some who thus received his influence wrote down a little clumsily what they remembered, and the things they wrote down, after so many catastrophes and such vast changes in Europe, stand to-day quite neat and clear. So that when you read of St. Louis it is like looking out of a little window, unglazed, in a tower, and seeing through it, framed in the stones of the wall, a well-ordered, sunlit landscape, particular, vivid, and defined; full of small brilliant things, exact in outline.

One day in that good thirteenth century, when all was new, amid the new white buildings, upon the new ordered roads, when even the grass was new (for it was Pentecost), the king, Louis the Saint, was in Corbeil with eighty of his knights and certain others of his train. And when he had eaten the morning meal (which was at nine o'clock, for that was their hour), he went down to the field below the chapel to speak at the door with Count John of Brittany, and with him was the Seneschal of Champagne and others, younger and older men. And as the groups stood there at the door in the spring sunlight, treading the spring grass, mown smooth, Robert of Cerbon (the same that founded the great college of Sorbonne, so that his name stands everywhere to-day for learning) took the young seneschal's coat and pulled him by it towards the king. And the seneschal said,—

"What would you with me, Master Robert?"

Robert said,—

"I wish to ask you this: If the king were to sit himself down in this field, and you were to sit down without leave on the same bench, and higher than he, would you not be to blame?"

"Yes," said the seneschal, "I should."

"Then," said Robert, "you are to blame now. For even now you are far more nobly clad than the king, for your coat is of many colours, and embroidered nobly with green, and the king does not go so clothed."

Louis, hearing this dispute, smiled at them but did not speak. And the seneschal answered sharply,—

"Master Robert, saving your grace, I am not to blame at all, though I do dress in 'broidery and in green. For this cloak was left to me by my father and my mother, who were noble. But you are to blame. For you are the son of a serf, and your mother was a serf as well, and you have given up the clothes that were left you by your father and your mother, and you are dressed in rich woollens much grander than the king's."

And the seneschal, growing livelier still, took Robert of Cerbon's coat, and took the hem of the king's coat, and held them up side by side, and said triumphantly,—

"There! See if I do not speak the truth. Look how much grander is the stuff you wear than the stuff that clothes the king."

Then King Louis spoke, and first he put his hand upon the sward and sat him down at the gate of the chapel, and said to his sons, who were there, young men,—

"Come, sit down beside me on the grass that we may hear each other the plainer."

And they answered,—

"Sire, we would not dare."

Then he said to the seneschal,—

"Seneschal, do you sit so."

And so did the seneschal. He sat so close that their two cloaks touched.

Then said St. Louis to his sons,—

"You have done very wrong in that you did not obey at once, you, my sons."

And then he said to the seneschal,—

"You did wrong to speak thus to Master Robert, and when I saw how shamed you made him, I at once knew that it was my business to defend him; and as to dress, this is my counsel: you all of you should dress well and decently, in order that your women may love you more, and that your household may respect you; for the wise man says that we ought to dress ourselves and to arm ourselves in such a manner that neither shall the good men of this world blame us for extravagance nor the young blades for meanness."

And upon another time, when they were sailing upon the sea, it being night, the ship was struck violently and lay over, and the storm rose so that it was thought she could not live. Then St. Louis, understanding that death was at hand, went as he was, half-clad, to where the Blessed Sacrament was kept, and there expected death.

But when the storm as suddenly abated, and the morning was come, and danger was passed, he asked by what name that wind was called which had nearly wrecked the King of France and all his people. To which the master mariner answered that this wind was no great wind, not one of the major winds of the world, not one of the cardinal winds, but a little side wind that hardly had a name, though some called it the little Gerbin wind.

When St. Louis heard this, he said to one of those about him,—

"See how great is God, and how He shows us His power. Since one of His little unimportant winds, which hardly has a name, all but destroyed the King of France, his children, and his wife, and all his household, in peril of the sea."

St. Louis, the king, loved also to tell this tale:—

There was a master in divinity, one who had disputed for the Faith, and he came to Bishop William of Paris in great distress, and said that he was full of doubt, and that his heart would not bend to believe in the Sacrament of the Altar, and that this mood, sent by the Enemy, pressed him sore.

To whom Bishop William answered,—

"And does this please you?"

To which the argufier answered vehemently,—

"Not at all! I am tormented thereby!"

"Sir," said the bishop again, "would you be pleased that these new doubts should conquer?"

"I would rather," said the poor man, "that my limbs should be torn from my body."

"Why, then," said Bishop William, "I will

give you a parable. You know that the King of France wars now with the King of England, and that on the front of this war stands the castle of Rochelle, which is in the country of Poitiers. Now, if the king had given you Rochelle to guard, upon the edges of the war where the fighting is, but to me the hill of Laon, peaceably in the heart of his kingdom, which would be honour most— to whom would he give the greater reward?"

"To the man," said the doubter, "who held Rochelle."

"Well, then," said Bishop William, "let me tell you that my heart is not even like the hill of Laon, but rather like the little hill of Montlheri, near Paris, with its tower, for I have never doubted at all. So where God gives me in reward one measure, he will give you four."

St. Louis said that one should never speak ill of any man, and those who listened closely to his talk never remembered his speaking ill of any man; on which account also he would never so much as mention the name of the Devil.

Also one day, when he was in Cyprus, on Crusade, he said to a companion that put water into his wine,—

"Why do you put water into your wine?"

Then that companion, who was a young man, answered,—

"For two reasons. First, because the physicians have warned me to do so; and secondly, because I do not wish to get drunk."

To which St. Louis answered,—

"You do well. For if you do not learn this custom in youth you will not practise it in age, and if in age you drink your wine unmixed, you will, without doubt, be drunk every evening of your life; which is a horrible thing to see in a valiant man."

And thinking of this, he said again,—

"Would you be honoured in this world, and then have Paradise?"

And the young man said "Yes."

Then the king said,—

"This is the rule: Neither say nor do what you would fear that all men should know."

And another time the king said to this young man, when they were on Crusade in the East,—

"Tell me which you would rather be—a leper, or in mortal sin."

And the young man, who was afraid to lie to the king, answered,—

"I would much rather have committed thirty or forty mortal sins than be a leper."

And the king did not answer him; but the next day he said to the young man,—

"Come here and sit at my feet." Which the young man did, and then St. Louis said, "You spoke yesterday like a wild man in a hurry, for all ills of the body are cured in a little time, when a man dies; but if your soul is tarnished, and you cannot be certain that God has pardoned you, that evil will last for ever as long as God sits in Paradise."

And then he asked the young man suddenly whether he ever washed the feet of poor men on Maundy Thursday, and the young man answered,—

"Sire, far be it from me to wash the feet of poor men! No! Never will I do this thing!"

And the king said to him,—

"You are wrong again—thinking yourself too grand to do what God did for our enlightenment. Now I pray you, for the love of God and for the love of me, get yourself into the habit of washing poor men's feet."

For this king loved all kinds of men, whatsoever kind God had made and Himself loved.

On which account also he would give castles to guard to men that had no claim on him, if they had renown in good deeds. And he would have at his table men of any birth for the same reason. And so seated once at table he said to a companion,—

"Tell me the reasons that a 'loyal gentleman' is so good a thing to be called."

Then they all began disputing and defining, and at the end the king said, giving no reasons and turning to Robert of Cerbon, the same whom he had defended for dressing well,—

"Master Robert, this is what I think upon the matter: I desire to be called by men a 'loyal gentleman,' but much more to know that I am one. And if you would leave me that, you might take all the rest; for that title is so great a thing, and so good a thing, that merely to name it fills my mouth."

THE DEATH OF ST. LOUIS

(*August* 25, 1270)

THERE is a little hill, not steep at first sight and seemingly very low, which rises bare enough to-day over the African Sea. The Mediterranean breaks (when in that sheltered gulf it breaks at all) in waves upon a straight and narrow beach at the foot of this hill. Beyond, not farther inland but farther up the coast, another hill, somewhat higher but still insignificant, is joined by a saddle to this first; to the south the land sinks altogether and admits (by a narrow passage) the sea into the broad and stagnant lagoon of Tunis.

A few isolated houses, with no pretense to comfort or to charm, a sort of villas, are to be found upon the quarter of mile of flat by the seashore, and one or two stand on the rise of the little height. Between them, for here a hundred yards and here two hundred, and all around them for half a mile and a mile again, is dry, burnt, dirty land, brown in summer, and empty save for here and there some tufts of coarse grass. Far off, in two great horns or arms leading to the horizon, run the mountain promontories that enclose this bay like a pocket—a side pocket of the sea. A tramway, come from Tunis and spanning the lagoon upon the embankment, runs past the base of the hill at the edge of the sea flat. There is a halt rather than a station, a deserted wooden platform without rooms or master. On that platform is the name of the place, "CARTHAGE"; and thus does a man to-day know where it was that the mighty Carthaginian aristocracy stood, where the ships rode innumerable, where Elissa died, and where the Roman armies, masters at last as armies always are of merchants and the sea, stormed yard by yard the rise to the Citadel.

It was upon this hill and near the summit of it, upon the eastern side which overlooks the water below, at a spot just in front of the place where the Saracens had built out of the blocks of Carthaginian ruin a castle of their own, that the King of France lay dying.

He was in his splendid tent, the baking air within hardly relieved by the lifting of its side and the spraying of water on the canvas. With him were his sons, and round that poor camp-bed were the many men of his house. It was the day after St. Bartholomew's feast, an awful day of heat in August, when the distant blue of the promontory hills trembled in the air, and when the iron of men's accoutrements, the rings of the saddle and of the bridle, were burning to the hand, and the baked earth of that low hill camp scorching to the feet.

St. Louis, who thus lay feeble in the last moments of his life, was but fifty-five years of age, nor did even these years fit him well, for his face had always something boyish in it and too tender for the approach of age. But the coming of death was clearly imprinted upon his pinched features, his lips without blood, and the droop of his mouth after so many days of pain. Before his voice fell low, while he yet had the power, he already had ordered a layer of ashes to be spread —as custom was then with pious rich men, that they might pass the more humbly. He said that Philip, his son, who was to reign after him, should be sent to him. This soldier was also weak from illness, but he came; and when that lord had come St. Louis said from his bed many things to this his heir, which things he ordered to be put down in writing as he spoke them, and to be kept as a testament for the governing of the realm of France, of which, years before, he had said to this same son as a child,—

"Rather would I that a Scot should come out of

Scotland to govern this land of France than that it should be governed other than in Christian wise."

Of these things which he gave for commandment to his son he said (among other things),—

"Fair son, the first thing I teach you is that you order your life to the love of God, for lacking this no man can be saved. If God sends you adversity, receive it in patience; if He sends you prosperity, give thanks humbly lest you become worse through pride. Confess thee often, and choose a wise confessor, who can guide you in what should be done, and what should be left undone; follow devoutly with heart and with lips the service of the Church, but especially the Mass, where Consecration is. Keep your heart soft and piteous to the poor, the misshapen, and all men ill at ease, and comfort and aid them within your power. Do not take all to which you have a right. If you have torment in your heart, share it with your confessor or some other man who is discreet. Thus will you bear it more easily. Cherish what is yours and your goods. Allow none to blaspheme God to your face. Be very stiff to insist on justice and on the fulfilment of rights, veering neither left nor right as between your subjects, and follow up the quarrel of the weak until full truth is declared. If you hold anything that you think another's, give it back at once, and if you are in doubt put the matter into the judgment of a third. Remember the chief townsfolk, for if you will rely on them, the foreigner and the great man within will fear to attack you. Revere your father and your mother in memory, and keep their commandments. Give the benefices of the Church not only to wise men but to clean. Do not fight against Christian men, at least without taking counsel, and in your wars spare the Church and all those who have done you no harm. Lastly, very dear son, have Masses sung for me for my soul, and prayers said throughout your realm, and I pray you put apart for this a fixed sum of all you receive. Dear and fair son, I give you all benedictions, whatever a good father can give his child, and may the Blessed Trinity and all the Saints guard and defend you from all evils, and God give you grace to do His will always, and to have Himself honoured by you so that you and I both, when we have done this mortal life, may be together with Him and praise Him for ever."

Then added King Louis, "Amen!"

But these are only certain few words out of all that St. Louis said, for the whole that he said was longer by far, and when he had done, it was the full heat of the day, and already he was failing.

The suffering he was in grew greatly. He called for the Sacraments. He received them with a whole mind, as was clearly apparent from this, that they could hear him murmuring the verses of the Psalms as they anointed him; and his younger son, the Count of Alençon, heard him as he whispered in death. He was calling in whispers upon the Saints, and in particular on St. James, the guardian of pilgrims and of men who take long voyages; also he called on St. Denis of France, and on St. Geneviève, who is the Queen of Paris, as all must know. But by this time, noon being long past, all strength was deserting him. He could make some sign, so that they lifted him as he desired down upon the bed of ash where he would pass; and lying there he found the strength to cross one hand above the other on his breast, and so lying backwards, and still looking up to Heaven, he gave up his spirit to God who made us, in that same hour of None—that is three o'clock in the afternoon, which is the hour in which God the Son died upon the Cross for the salvation of the world.

Thus, upon the morrow of the Feast of St.

Bartholomew the Apostle, passed wholly out of this world the good King Louis, in the year of the Incarnation of our Lord, the year of Grace 1270. And his bones were put into a chase and buried at St. Denis in France, there in the place where he had chosen his sepulchre. In which place he was laid away in earth, there where God has worked many a miracle for him through his deserts.

THE TEMPLARS

IN that quarter of Paris which lay to the north, built on the old marsh that had been so laboriously drained, and close to the wall which Philip Augustus had thrown round the city a century before, stood wide, with its open spaces and innumerable roofs, the enclosure of the Templars. It was a polity within a polity. No thoroughfare ran through those many acres, and gates admitted outsiders through the walls just as gates similarly guarded admitted outsiders through the walls into that larger unit of the city.

This fortification of stone all about, this high curtain flanked with towers and containing within its defences a whole population, was the very symbol of what the Temple had become. Wherever Christian men (now that the Crusades had failed) still held their own against the pressure of Baltic heathendom or of Islam insolent upon the east and south, there the Temple, over wide estates or commanding great castles armed, boasted its power.

Within the fields of Christendom, far within, wherever long immunity from heathen or from

Saracen pressure had half corrupted the life of
Christian men, the Temple boasted its wealth or
exalted its luxury.   In London, in Ravenna, in
Aragon—principally here in Paris—everywhere
it was the richest and the greatest thing.   Christendom counted perhaps one hundred thousand
manors; nine thousand were in the hands of the
Temple.   Saving perhaps the Papacy itself, the
enormous wealth of the Jewish financiers, and the
Courts of the Angevins and of the Capetians,
there was no such strength of gold anywhere in
Europe.   It was the rival of all of these, and I
think their superior.

And this vast Order, as it was thus so enormously strong through gold, was strong also
through two other things—ubiquity and noble
lineage; and through a third thing it was strong
—secrecy.   For those younger sons of the great
nobles, those many squires and those knights returned from wars in Spain or in the Levant, who
formed its not very numerous but dominating
body, were bound by so strict a discipline and
acted with such solidarity behind their fortress
gates in every capital and garrison, that it seemed
as though Christendom had now within it some
alien body separate from itself, and already half
an enemy to the great traditions of the common

people and of the universal Church, and of those
open public servants, the kings. There was a
grumbling and a hatred against Templars everywhere. It had endured for fifty years. What
was all this wealth and all this secrecy? Of what
sort was the evil that hid behind those walls? And
how could there be tolerated in Christendom,
whose nature it is to be both homogeneous and
free, something so jealously separate and possessed of such unaccredited dominion?

And more: were not these men, by the very
tenure of their office, the defenders of the Holy
Sepulchre, and had not that charge of theirs
been lost? St. Peter men knew, and his suc-
cessor, and the kings they knew, and the great
lords their barons; but what was this other thing
established in their midst, irresponsible and giving
no man account of their worship—whatever it
was they worshipped? Some said it was an idol.
All feared it was Satan. The great Orders, the
preachers coming right out of the populace,
mixing with them, and haranguing in the market-
places, were no such peril. The Jews, in the mass
small men and poor, some few composing that
strong oligarchy of finance which had long domi-
nated Europe, were exposed to constraint; but
even those that hated them could jest with them.

They were neighbours. The pitiless executors of royal orders were still neighbours too. Whatever had power for whatever reasons over the lives of common men was at least known and openly judged—save only the Temple. All the West in the great mass of its people was inflamed and alarmed, the little children playing in the street put forth their fingers to ward off bad influence whenever two Templars went by. Men loved to repeat whatever tales were told against them; and the pride of their demeanour, sprung from a general nobility of blood as much as from the consciousness of unchallenged strength, exasperated the public soul.

Of all such angers the Capetian monarchy was about to become the spokesman. It was a rôle perilous in the extreme; for to strike at such a thing a man must strike at once with a secrecy equal to its own and with a power almost as universal. Time and again, for a generation past, it had been said that the thing would be done. Philip the Fair, King of France, discovered in his jealousy, and perhaps in his indignation, the strength required for the blow.

*   *   *   *   *

That fortress, which stood, an isolated thing,

challenging the greater fortress which Paris was,
had in its centre, overlooking the many low gables
of its outhouses and servants of those who lived
under its protection, of its guests, and of its
treasure rooms, one great square tower, capped
with the high, pointed slate roof which could be
seen from miles around. The tower was as tall
and as menacing as the huge round tower of the
Louvre itself; it lifted above Paris as high as the
old belfry of St. Germanus, or as the twin praying
towers of Notre-Dame.

Within that tower certain men, among the
chiefs of the whole Order, sat upon an autumn
evening, feasting. It was a Friday in October,
and Friday is a day big with the superstitions or
the disasters of Christendom. It was in October,
the 13th of the month, and thirteen is a number
which Christendom has consented to regard with
some similar dread.

But these men suffered no great fear, although
so much had been rumoured now year after year.
The greater part of them had come to Paris upon
the invitation of the king but recently. That
Burgundian squire, who was the chief of them
all, had only the day before walked, by the king's
own order, in a funeral of the king's own Court,
holding the pall and playing his great part.

Certain of these men, the lesser ones, spoke as they sat at meat in this high tower, which in a fashion commanded the city, of the talk that was everywhere about, and the dangers which all might feel to be in the air they breathed. But their timorous suggestions were ridiculed both by the gayer of their colleagues and by the grave reproof of the superiors who sat there eating and drinking with them.

It was not yet quite dark, for this meal of the day was a meal begun at five o'clock as we now reckon time.

"There is such power in the Temple," said that Burgundian knight, the old Grand Master, gravely, "that if there were but allied with them those others of the Knights Hospitallers which are not of our body, freely could they rule the whole world."

Then another said, after a little pause,—

"Though the King of France himself should seek to do us some evil, others as powerful as he would stand our sponsors. The King of Aragon was with us when last the dogs growled and dared not bite."

Then a third, who had a subtle face and spoke in a high voice, said, not pleasantly,—

"Were my own father to seek admission to this

Order of ours I would warn him that there are
things known to us which should bid him pause,
for there are secrets we hold" (and here he
smiled at the brethren) "which are known only
to God and to the Devil—and to you: three
partners."

As the last man said this, the youngest of the
Templars there present showed in his face at once
so great a terror and so great a pain that the
speaker sneered. That young man was muttering to himself. The Grand Master, speaking still
gravely but somewhat sharply from his old lips,
asked him what words he was thus saying
secretly.

"I was praying to the Mother of God," said
the young man, "and I was thinking of the
dead."

From the streets below, as evening gathered,
there came a sound perhaps a little louder than
the common sound of the tradesmen at their
booths and of the passing crowds, but not much
louder. Over the river, in the king's garden
under the new white walls and squat turrets of
the palace on the island, a strange gathering had
met. There assembled at the king's express command members chosen from all the guilds and
trades of Paris. They sat in rank, some hundreds

in number, by parishes and by mysteries beneath certain wooden pulpits that had been hastily set up; and, from these, monks of the preaching Orders cried out in tones of violence and of condemnation, preparing them for what was to come.

"A thing deplorable and horrible to the mind is among us, and a thing terrible to the ears. . . . Natures that have exiled themselves beyond the bounds of nature, treasonable to the dignity of man. Christ is betrayed, and their initiation is the initiation of devils. They spit upon the Cross."

Also to these men admissions made by Templars who had betrayed their Order were related, and truth and rumour, and blasphemy and justice, were commingled in these high denunciations.

The congregation of these picked men chosen to spread the thing immediately throughout Paris were ready to believe, and most of what they believed was true.

But still in that high tower, as the darkness came, the chiefs of the Templars were confident and immune. Nothing in Christendom was so strong as they. The noise from the streets beyond their walls grew less, then suddenly rose and

was more ordered and, as it were, more menacing,
They could catch the regular footfall of men in
rank and the clank of metal. Some rose, and
going to the deep western windows of their high
place, whence the sunset beyond Valerian and
the hills of St. Cloud still warmed all the sky,
they saw torches lit in the gloaming, and they
heard a challenge at the gate. The gate opened,
and a troop poured in. It was the king's men.

No resistance was held or opposed. That
great door of the tower itself, which was to stand
as the tower stood for so many centuries more
(until it fell at the orders of Napoleon), was
opened to the order of the king. The men who
opened it at first looked at one another. None
spoke save the Grand Master, who only said,
"Woe to him that betrays his brethren," and
who, as he said it, looked fixedly at the youngest
man. Then the worked hanging, which hung
by rings before the archway of their room, was
drawn clattering aside. The archers entered in
a body, and these men were prisoners. Before
it was night Philip himself, the king, had taken
possession of that tower. He had filled it with
his scribes. The treasury was forced. The rolls
of parchment were brought forth, the accounts
were rendered, and the vast fortunes of that place

were beneath the grasp of the monarchy, which would proceed to the full revelation of so many crimes and of the humbling of so much pride, to the torture and to the death.

But later, months and months later, when the last of these men were themselves brought out for public recantation before the cathedral, the old Grand Master, that Burgundian knight, standing forward on the high platform before the thousands of the people to declare the guilt of the Templars to the astonishment of Europe, for all his avowals acted a most memorable part. Loudly he denied whatever wrongs he had himself admitted, whatever blasphemies, whatever obscenities, whatever denials of the Christ. They burnt him with his companions after that relapse (for so they called it); they burnt him on those little islands which lay westward of the palace, and which are now a green place beneath the Place Dauphine; and the awestruck crowd that watched his death whispered among themselves that the man in his agony had summoned to the tribunal of God within one year and a day the Pope and the King. Before the term of that citation had expired the Pope and the King were dead.

BLANCHETAQUE

(Augu∫t 24, 1346)

[*I have corre∂ed Froissart by the map and local knowledge.
Hence Boismont, not Oisemont, etc.*]

EDWARD THE PLANTAGENET sat in
Boismont at his evening meal upon Wednesday, August 23, 1346. He, and his nobles about
him. He had marched from Acheux that day,
an easy journey. He had found at Boismont,
before sunset, the advance guard of his force;
now, by evening, it had all concentrated, and the
division (as we should call it to-day, for it was
about that strength) lay, some in bivouac, some
billeted, some under canvas, grouped round the
village. The moon was at the full; through the
late summer air, still warm, the flood of her light
was over those miles of stubble, the open high
fields of Picardy.

Edward the Plantagenet, in a chance room of
the village, chosen in its best house, still sat at a
table well furnished and spoke to those about
him of the campaign.

There sat among these who were that night
the guests of the king one or two useful upland

squires, a little doubtful of their French, a little
afraid, therefore, of speaking in such company;
but Edward could understand, and could even
make himself understood in the local idioms of
north England which sounded so harsh in such
a place; and, intermingled with the play of French
at that table—with the advice and the jests and
the courtesy of the greater men—he would demand the opinion and listen carefully to the reply
of those few whom he had also bidden to meet
him, and who, in their ignorance, hesitated to
use the tongue of their rank.

But there was little to learn, either from these
few who were easier in their half-Saxon dialects,
or from the main group of guests with whom, as
with the king, French was the only talk. The
position was known, its character was simple, its
issue was desperate.

Headquarters take tragedy in war with a
strange ease, partly because it is their duty to
check emotion, partly because they have to handle
affairs as a problem in the void, and to forget the
too human reactions of peril; partly because they
have grown too familiar with an evil situation,
if that situation has arisen gradually and en-
forced itself; partly because instruction, and the
habit of a cultured class, has taught them how

futile in such a pass is any waste of energy upon grieving.

In the billets and posts around, the polyglot gossip at the camp fires and hearths, where sergeants saw to the cooking of the common meals, was less restrained; and in Welsh, and in the Saxon or nearly English phrases, in the rare French, in the mingled speech of the men from the sea coast, there was a note always of gloom and sometimes of alarm. Though the solid organization of the sergeants saw to it that the muttering should not spread too far, there could be no mistaking the temper of the troops. They knew, by that curious unexplained process through which the common soldier absorbs a position which he could not understand from a map, that things were desperate.

But around the king's table a much clearer appreciation of the peril led to no corresponding words, nor would any stranger present have imagined, from the tone of that room, how close and apparently inevitable was disaster.

The little force had now been in retreat, and rapid retreat, from the failure before Paris, through one feverish week, pounding up northward for Calais; not with forced marches, indeed, but with full days' marches. Now, at the end of that effort, it found itself headed off. The long, straight, marshy trench of the Somme lay between them and their Channel transports home. They had attempted its crossing a first, a second, a third time, and every attempt had been thrust back. They had felt down river with increasing anxiety, as the host upon the farther bank grew; and, while they had failed to make the crossing good, and while, as they were thus impelled northward, the breadth of the valley which defied them increased. Here they were at last at Boismont, on the lower estuary, with a huge sea tide swirling back and forth, at its height—a mile and a half of deep tumbling water—twice the depth that would drown a man. At its lowest it became a mass of marsh and mud, through which the hurrying ebb ran tumbling to the sea in varied channels.

Boismont stood upon the eastern bank of that broad water flank, grouped upon the dry steep above the edge of the marsh and the mud. There were rumours of some available passage, but no one caught sight of it, and even were it known, what chance had the army of forcing a long and narrow and perilous traverse when they had been unable to force the short bridges of the upper stream?

Yet that very difficulty was to prove their salvation. There was a ford, as the king was to learn, but its farther end upon the eastern bank was ill guarded with an insufficient force detached from the French vanguard upon the farther shore. For it was imagined that the crossing could hardly be attempted, or, if attempted, easily repelled.

Edward Plantagenet turned to one of the lesser commanders, who had spoken of the rumour of a ford, and said,—

"What was the name of your prisoner?"

The soldier replied,—

"Gobain Agache. He is a farmer of Mons, through which we marched but yesterday. We took him with us because he had been talking too much."

"One might have thought that you could have found intelligence."

"No, sir; they were all dumb. But we had heard that this man had talked, so we took him with us."

"What has he told you?"

"He has told us nothing."

"What have you offered him?"

The commander mentioned a sum large in his eyes. Edward Plantagenet laughed.

"We will give him the worth of his whole farm," he said, "and his freedom, and that of any twenty of his comrades. Are there so many from his part?"

"No doubt, sir," said the officer.

They sent for Gobain Agache, and they made him their offer pleasantly enough. He stood before them stolid for a moment. They did not press him.

As to which of these two kings should prove himself by ordeal of battle to be the rightful king Gobain Agache cared nothing. The jabbering of Welsh and of half English in the billets had sounded to him very foreign indeed, but then many of the others there were also of his own kind. He was disturbed in the matter of loyalty to his lord, who, he was told, had followed the Valois king upon the farther side of the river. He was disturbed about his farm, and what would happen to it if the battle were decided one way or the other; and here he was, with the value of his farm to his hand for the taking! So he spoke.

"The ford is close by. Your men ought to have seen it. Any stranger could see it. It is clearly marked at low tide from the hard to the hard, a broad made way of marl and chalk and great stones going right across the river."

Edward looked at that one of his subordinates chiefly responsible, who murmured at once,—

"Sir, we did not reach this bank until the tide was already flowing."

"Did you see a hard going down into the water?" said the king sharply.

"I thought it was a village wharf."

The king smiled, and turned again to Gobain Agache.

"How broad is it?"

"About twenty paces," said the farmer.

"Who is the best fisherman here?" said the king abruptly.

Gobain hesitated.

"I do not know the place," he said.

The king nodded his head slightly to a younger man who stood ready. That younger man went out. Edward bade the farmer be seated on a form near the wall, and spent the next few minutes talking of this and that at random, until the young man who had gone out came back with an old, wooden-faced fellow, who pulled his hair as he entered and stood stooping somewhat and stroking his beard with his left hand.

Of him the king asked at what o'clock the tide was full. He said, but in the speech of St. Valery,—

"At midnight, for it is the full moon."

"That means that the last of the ebb," said

Edward, half to himself and half to his companions, "will be a little after six in the morning."

The fisherman shook his head and grinned at
hearing such strange errors.

"After seven," he said. "Seven hours ebb,
five hours flow."

An old man, half servant, half vassal, who
looked after the king's land round the waters of
Chichester harbour, and who could always be
straight with his master, looked him full in the
face and said,—

"Never argue about the tide."

And Edward answered,—

"All the better, so long as it is not too late."

Then he turned to the old fisherman for a last
question,—

"What depth is there at the very lowest of the
passage on this ebb?"

"No more than knee-deep water," said the old
man, "for the springs are making, and we shall
have the lowest ebb in three more tides."

All this the king fitted together in one. He
saw his opportunity. The ford close at hand, its
hardness, the chance of the tide just at the right
moment; he saw how all depended upon the
defence of the farther shore. He saw that his

chance of crossing and escaping to Calais had come.

He told the young man to lead the fisherman out and to give him a piece of gold, and to see that no one took it from him.

*   *   *   *   *

The king gave orders for a march in the first hours of the morning, long before dawn, while still they had the full moonlight to guide them. The sergeants were warned. The Court and the army took but little sleep. The grooms had none.

The accustomed delays and rearrangements, without which no force is gathered, kept them to within two hours of dawn. There was but one road leading parallel to the shore along the higher dry land southward; the very long column followed it under the moonlight. They reached Saigneville, those few miles to the south, just as the beginnings of daylight, mixing in with the last gold of the moon, was restoring colour to the world. Yet an hour more was the division occupied in marshalling under three columns to face the river. It was broad daylight by the time everything was done, and the sun was very near the edge of the uplands on the farther shore.

In front of the army ran rapidly the broad
stream of the estuary, racing at more than half
ebb to the sea. Already the mud flats below the
village were widely exposed, and were similarly
showing upon the farther bank, and there, running out boldly to the water, which still sub-
merged it, was the causeway of the ford. Its pro-
longation, now that they knew its character, could
be caught by the eye nearly a mile beyond, upon
the farther flats. It was Blanchetaque, the ford,
broad and raised as Gobain had described it. Far
away upon the low bluff there could just be made
out doubtfully the small—the too small—force
which the advance guard of the Valois had sent to
protect that scarcely threatened issue. It num-
bered not a sixth of the Plantagenet's columns.

Those three columns waited for the fall of the
tide. Before them, in a small, close group, some
four hundred knights, fully armed, stood for the
order to mount. It came somewhat before seven
in the morning. The thing had to be calculated
closely. Too early a start would find unfordable
water. Too late would mean the catching of the
ends of the column by the tide; for the rearguard
of that army, as it crossed on so narrow a front,
was two miles from the head.

The signal sounded, and that trumpet was

heard by Godemard de Fay, the commander of the Valois on the farther bank. He saw Edward's knights mount, and the three columns, each four abreast, coming across the covered causeway, formed. Against Edward's mounted squires he sent knights, equally mounted and armed, down into the water to take the shock. These two small bodies of cavalry met, struggling and thrusting and hacking at each other, with the salt ebb swirling round the horses' knees as the beasts slipped and struggled on the slime of the causeway floor. But not the wrestling between those handfuls of heavily accoutred nobles was to decide the passage. That was determined by the long-bow.

Behind the French knights, on the hard above the falling water level, a detachment of the Genoese with their cross-bows supported the horse and sent their shafts into the mass of Edward's knights, perhaps just reaching the infantry behind. But that infantry was here in the van, wholly made up of the archers, the superb arm of all that command, and it was *they* who forced the advance. For the Welsh long-bow, with its greater precision, its sharper impact, its longer range, and the discipline of the force that used it, firing with exactitude and command, not only threw Godemard's horse into a confusion, stampeding from the causeway into the mud and breaking back towards the shore, but threw into an equal confusion the Genoese archers and the French infantry behind. Edward's knights, acting as a sort of spearhead, could go forward, but only through the perpetual support of the longbow men as they advanced steadily through the narrowing water and up towards the shore.

There was a moment of hesitation and of last resistance, then that break in the line which is the end. Edward could see from far off the horse of his small group of knights vigorously mounting the bluff, and the scattering of the small force that opposed them. The bridgehead was held; the main army began to file across.

So close was the issue that it could hardly save its baggage. A detachment of the King of France's forces had already appeared upon the sky-line above Saigneville before the wagons could follow the last of the English infantry on to the ford. Much of Edward's train had to be abandoned. But that same accident which caused so severe a loss in provision saved the army. The Plantagenet's command, nearly all its fighting men at least, had crossed the Somme, and the rising tide had made pursuit impossible by the time the Valois' men had made secure of their booty and had reached the eastern bank. They watched the growing flood of water between, as, far away upon the farther bank, the triple column of the English king disappeared over the western folds of the land.

This was the crossing of Blanchetaque, and this it was which founded, two days later, the decision of Crécy.

Edward had said "God and our Lady and St. George will find me a passage."

VILLE GAGNÉE

IN Paris never was such confusion of mind, such exhaustion of argument! It had gone on for twenty years, for twenty-one years—and you would have said that no man knew where he stood. For who was king? And where stood Burgundy? And what had come of what had been the Armagnacs? Never was such a generation of conflict since the city had been founded!

There are two currents in such turmoils: the young men, and the fathers. Now the young men, from those of thirty who could just remember the news of Agincourt, and who, in their teens, had seen the great massacres when the Burgundians had retaken the city from the Armagnacs, had lived all their lives under a king—the grandson of a king of France, the son of a daughter of France—but a king also of England, and himself a child whom they hardly saw. Still, that was their king. Their priests, their notables, their magistrates—all the world about them, took such a king for granted, and Burgundy, that great house which the populace of Paris had always loved to follow, still swore by such a king. The old men would some of them remember this child-king as a usurper, but some of them as a restoration of good things; for was not this new Plantagenet kingship the work of Burgundy and the end of the hateful Armagnac? Was it not a true Parisian thing?

All the great story of Joan, those intense two years, had not passed unheeded. The loud echoes of it had sounded through Paris on that memorable day when the armoured girl had fallen wounded in the fruitless assault upon the St. Honoré Gate. But not even that great sweep of reconquest could wholly shake the city. All the country round fell away from the Plantagenet to the Valois, but Paris was still Plantagenet. For nearly half a lifetime one state of things had endured, and after so many miseries it seemed well enough.

But latterly there had come a change. For the people, and especially the young men, were telling each other that Burgundy was no longer friends with their boyish, weak, and distant king; and at the same time had come a petty but significant alteration in the air of the city, something that the men of the time hardly noticed—some-

thing of profound significance for posterity was
at work. The forces within the city were no
longer of one kind. Even of the nobles, some
were wholly foreign. The English tongue had
arisen, and Willoughby, in command of the garrison, was of that tongue. The conqueror of
Agincourt had spoken, thought, and lived in
French. It was as a man indistinguishable from
their own nobles that he had ridden all the way
down the narrow St. Martin's street, kissing the
relics at the church doors when he made his
entry into Paris, all those years before. But even
by his time the tide had turned in England. The
Black Death had done its work before he was
born. Henry V. himself could use the English
tongue, and to all the lesser men about him it
was native. Many nobles even could then speak
no other. Now, after the working of a full
seventeen years, the estrangement was more pronounced still; and the populace of Paris knew
not, when a patrol passed by at night, whether
its few men would chance to be men of like speech
with themselves or of alien tongue.

And there was yet another matter, perhaps
decisive of the issue that came—in part because
a reliance upon Burgundy had made the populace
seem secure for the young Plantagenet king, in

part because the heavy drain of men in the losing campaign all around left few to spare for Paris: *the garrison in arms under Willoughby was too small*—hardly more than a battalion (as we say to-day) and a couple of squadrons.

Already by the spring of the year the regency of England and of France was troubled, and a month before Easter the citizens had been summoned to take oath, individually, in support of that treaty of Troyes by which the young king reigned. For his mother, a princess of the blood royal of France, was dead. Very few refused to swear. All the great notables swore. The Bishop and the Abbots and the Prior of St. Martin, and the chiefs of all the Courts of Justice and of the Exchequer, and all the Bar, and all the City Companies, and every priest and monk. It seemed a unanimity; though some few had taken advantage of the liberty to leave the town, if their allegiance was to him, the Valois, who called himself King of France outside the walls.

Beneath that official surface the quarrel between the government at Westminster and Burgundy had changed the Parisian mind. Already, secretly, letters were passing between a little group of the livery-men of the city and Charles of Valois, the king who was reconquering his kingdom. They treated for amnesty; they assured Charles (with too much assurance) that he had the support of the populace in the streets.

So passed Easter. Arthur of Brittany, Count of Richemont and Constable of France, received those letters and made his plan. No very great force accompanied him as he marched up northwards towards Paris through the night, but from within the city there was nothing strong enough to meet him. There is a curious air of ease, simplicity, and silence about that last revolution which suddenly slipped the great capital away from the hands of the Lancastrian Plantagenets, kings of England.

They had marched, I say, through the night. Richemont the Constable, and Dunois with him: Dunois, who had been through all those battles with Joan, and was now to see their last fruit fall ripe into his hands.

It was the morning of Friday, the Friday after Easter, the 13th of April, 1436, just at dawn. The two flanking towers of St. Michael's Gate, the southern gate of the city, stood clear in the new light, just before the rising of the sun. The grey of their old stones, and of their old slate, pointed, conical roofs (for the new wall covered only the north of the city, and in the south the old wall remained), was marked in every detail, and against the sky stood one man mounting guard upon the parapet.

Henry of Villeblanche, a gentleman of Brittany, bore the white lilies, the banner of the Valois, by the Constable's side. Him did Richemont send forward to challenge the guard, and to him that lonely man upon the parapet gave the simple answer: "Not this gate, the next." Such was the mood of the garrison. The commanders rode round, certain that none would challenge. They came to St. James's Gate, little more than a bowshot away to the east; the postern was opened to him. He sent through a handful of his men; the men of the guard looked on, neither aiding nor resisting. The newcomers broke the links of the drawbridge chain and the heavy gangway came down with a clang, bridging the ditch. Across it rode at once the Constable and Dunois, then Philip of Ternaut, the fourth a plain knight, Simon of Lallain, and behind them the little force of men-at-arms and grooms, hardly two thousand all told, filed under the dark ogive archway and on into the city street, which pointed with its old Roman straightness right down the hill to the island. As they so rode L'Isle-Adam, the Marshal, climbed up the winding stair behind the guardroom to the top of the gate, carrying with him the flag of the lilies, the flag of the Valois. He ran it up in the growing morning light, and cried out, *"Ville gagnée!"* Never was there an odder capture of any walled strong city, famous throughout the world.

That troop of horse went on down the hill and through the streets in turn to the island, to the cathedral, to the town hall, to the market. The townsmen were just astir; few took heed. The Constable, he and his men, rode back to the cathedral again—Notre-Dame—and, leaving the horses outside, four to a groom, they dismounted in their full armour and heard the early morning Mass all together; and the canons who had so recently sworn for the rival king received them. But as the priests offered food, after the Mass, the Constable answered, "I hold the custom of fasting on a Friday, and I shall eat nothing." As they came out from the great church the alarm was already raised. The little garrison was afoot, and Willoughby, at the head of it, raised the official part of the city. No one knew at that hour what would follow. All was still in doubt.

It was the populace, not the two opposing troops, which took the shock. It rose in a sudden tide, turned by we know not what preparatory workings of the last few weeks, or perhaps by a gusty mood. A group of unarmed men, running up to the northern gate, seized the cannon there, four or five small pieces, turned them down the street, and just as they did so saw Willoughby coming up with his little column of horse and foot. A volley of round shot pulled up Willoughby with some loss and turned him back.

The official world failed to raise a force. The leaders of the merchants, the greater lawyers coming into the street and shouting for King Henry, the bishops themselves, two of whom had begun to harangue, all failed; and the mob, growing greater street by street, shut off the issues with chains and ran back to attack Willoughby's men-at-arms with anything that came to hand. That soldier kept his small troop well together, and through the increasing flood made eastward down St. Anthony's Street to the Bastille. He had hardly twelve hundred men with him, counting both the French and the English-speaking sort, all told. He shut himself up in the Bastille, having saved his command. There he awaited terms.

The Constable at once organized the city: put garrisons to all the gates, had convoys of wheat brought in, and a market opened at once; put men of his own at the town hall and over the city companies, strongly holding all that merchant class which was the foundation of the Plantagenet power; he proclaimed the decree of his master, the French king, Charles—a decree of general amnesty—and all the Saturday organized the city and brought it to order. On Sunday, the 15th, he prepared to establish his lines round the Bastille with troops whom he had sent for from the neighbouring garrisons outside the town. Willoughby asked for terms, and generous terms were granted. The council round the Constable demanded that the Bastille be handed over to Ternaut; as for Willoughby himself and his men and his civilian notables, they should be convoyed safely, not through the now hostile streets, but round by the north, outside the new city wall.

As they passed, the men from the wall insulted them, and particularly that Bishop of Therouenne, who had been chancellor for the late government, to whom they called out, *"Ah, the fox! The fox!"* But he grumbled, not at the insult but at the loss of his jewels, and no man heeded him. Just behind the Louvre, where the city wall ended at the water, and where the footbridge runs to-day across the river, they embarked that little force to go down the Seine to Rouen, honourably enough. And so ended the rule of the Plantagenets in Paris.

LOUIS XI AND CHARLES THE BOLD

(*January* 5, 1477)

IN a small room, the large grey stones of whose walls were partly hidden under tapestries, there sat at evening a man too wizened to show his full age. He was in the fifties. He might have been fifteen years younger or fifteen years older—he would have looked the same. He was simply dressed—it was winter—in warm grey clothes, and though a great fire of logs burnt in the huge open hearth of the small room, he had a thick cloak over his shoulders. He was cold, and thrust forward to the flames long, thin and somewhat grasping hands. His keen, narrow eyes, closely set together and very bright, shone in the firelight. On a large oak table to his left stood carefully ranged a mass of papers, and one great parchment which he had been consulting. But for the moment he read nothing. He muttered to himself.

One soldier was in the room, standing silent by the curtain which hid the door. Without could be heard from time to time the metallic clinking of arms and the steps of men coming and returning. At long intervals there came from distant roofs of the castle the cry of the sentry. For the rest there was no sound in that room save the crackling of the fire and the continued muttering of this man.

It was the king—Louis XI.

To his hand there upon the table, and docketed and filed minutely, stood his immediate affairs; accurately, in shelves which lined the larger rooms of the castle, and served by a great staff of clerks, was further stored the whole business of the realm.

In his childhood that realm was ruined. As a little frail child of five he had seen Joan passing through his father's palace at Bourges. In his boyhood had come the difficult reconquest; his manhood had been filled with exiles, with quarrels against his father, the reigning king, and with a long apprenticeship in intrigue.

It was his business to rebuild the realm. And for now nearly sixteen years he had plunged into that business as private men of the same sort will plunge into the accumulation of a fortune. It had absorbed him altogether, and his soul, never sane, had suffered from that absorption, much as suffer the souls of men who devote themselves in the same fashion to gold.

But his zeal was for the re-establishment of the realm. This, the unceasing pressure of a spirit which for centuries had urged and spurred the Capetian line, which had made them—some quite unconsciously, none quite consciously—the agents of a great purpose, had urged Louis continually. His task was nearly done. Only one great rival still loomed to the east of him. It was Burgundy.

All that Rhineland, all that great street from south to north, from the Alps to the Low Countries, all that belt of true French soil, and of its extension into the Germanies, was under a man— Charles the Bold—ten years younger than himself, who, building on his father's power, had dared to conceive independence. He would make a new State, breaking the vassalage with the King of France. He would leave France halved.

This man, Charles, stood against that older man, Louis, in a contrast more complete than any two rivals you can name: Louis frail, cunning, tenacious, garrulous, delighting in a millioned web of detail, patient, cruel, diseased: Charles, short but strong in the saddle, square-shouldered, violent in action, somewhat silent, his mass of thick black hair ponderous upon his enormous head, living in the midst of charges, and thinking that the world could be carried at a charge.

The last issue between these two men had come. The one was sitting here in his narrow room, in the heart of France, holding the threads which stretched to the ends of Europe. The other, in camp, pursued the siege of Nancy, and was in the act of taking that capital, destroying Lorraine: confirming his power.

*   *   *   *   *

As King Louis sat there, his hands and feet toward the flame, muttering to himself, and his bright, narrow eyes seeing scheme after scheme conjointly in the dancing of the fire, his mood suddenly changed and, as though he were alone, careless of the attendant, he suddenly threw himself upon his knees at the chair where he had been sitting, and raised his mutterings somewhat into prayers. He groped in his breast for an amulet and kissed it fervently, and continued in a litany name after name of those who should protect him and his race, and all his land. But the name which occurred most often in that confused torrent of intense mumbling was the name of St. Martin of Tours, his neighbour, his protector, he to whom Louis the King had shown such generosity; he upon whom Louis the King had showered so much wealth, and before whom he continued to bow.

*   *   *   *   *

In the first light of a very cold morning the king rode out with half a dozen familiars. He was helped with difficulty not on to a horse but on to a mule. His long, thin, somewhat deformed legs with difficulty held the saddle, and he stooped forward gracelessly as he rode. No one could have told him from a chance traveller of the poorer sort. He was in grey, as always—a thick, coarse cloth—and on his head a rough, pointed hat, with a leaden medal stuck in the band of it, and on the medal, stamped, an image of Our Lady.

He rode out over the drawbridge toward Tours, in the bitterly cold mist as the day broadened. One hundred yards and more behind came the archers and the drivers of the wagons; for he had begun a journey.

The king and his little group of attendants halted for twenty minutes in the town for Mass. As he came out of Mass, he turned to the first poor inn of the market square, and ate the first short meal of the day, while the innkeeper and the serving-maid watched him in terror, and the passers-by in the streets huddled in corners, catching glimpses of him through the thick, small panes of the window.

And all during that meal he talked, and talked incessantly, to his companions, upon every point of his policy: upon the place they should visit, upon the chances of meeting the messenger whom he expected—upon all things.

They took the road again like a little company of poor pilgrims; they followed up the Loire.

They came at last to a place where the road, damp with melting snow but now lit by a pale morning sun, passed through a deep wood along the river bank, and there stood a hut which the foresters used. It was the appointed spot. The king halted, dismounted, and entered with but one companion. The rest stood without.

They had not long to wait. Another small group approached from the west, but these were splashed with mud, broken with fatigue, their fine horses hardly carrying them, and stumbling as they went. One of them was half in armour, and seemed to be their chief. He scrambled down stiffly from his beast, almost falling as he did so, entered the hut, and knelt before the king.

The king raised him, but before he could tell

his great news Louis deluged him with yet another river of talk. How were the ways? What
had he met? Had he passed through Bar, or
had he come round north through Argonne?
Had he heard what the common people were
saying in either place?

Twice the newcomer attempted to tell his news,
and twice he was swamped again by that ceaseless
flood of clipped, tumbling words. At last he had
his moment, and he took it to tell in three phrases
the enormous thing which he had carried in silence
through that night and through four desperate
marches before.

Charles the Bold was dead. Nancy was relieved. Lorraine was master of his own again.
The imagined new State was in ruins. Louis
took up the ceaseless chatter again, patting the
hand of his messenger as he did so, and smiling
a thin but contented smile.

His work was accomplished. His great scheme
was fulfilled, and yet such a moment led him to
nothing more solemn than an endless cataract
of words—save for one moment, when he fell
again upon his knees on the earth floor of that
hut and prayed as fervently as though he had
been alone. He rose again to question and re-

question, and to make his comments. He was
exhausted before he was silent.

* * * * *

Meanwhile, far off in Lorraine, the battle had
been brought to its conclusion, and the great
Duke was dead.

It was upon Sunday, the 5th of January 1477,
that René of Lorraine, coming out from his Mass
in the Abbey Church of St. Nicholas, had ordered
his armies—some few of the lords of the Barrois,
some few more from the Charolais, some from
the Jura were there; but the great mass of his
rank and file were a hubbub of German talk from
the Alsatian towns and from the Swiss mountains—ten thousand of them.

They had not far to go. Nancy was but a
short two hours' march away, and there, before
his capital, starving and on the edge of surrender,
Lorraine knew that the way was barred by the
army of Charles.

It had been bitter cold, but there was half a
thaw. The ice on the Meurthe (to the right of
the road as the long column went northward
up the bank) was still continuous, but thin and
slushy. The great masses of snow round about
were melting. It was somewhat before noon

that they saw, drawn up in rank upon slightly rising ground before them, the host of Charles, and in the distance behind it, two miles away, the spires of Nancy.

From a wood upon his right to the west, down to the river Meurthe upon the east, Charles had drawn his line, with his guns commanding the road whereby the columns of Lorraine should advance. Fine snow began to fall, and under the veil of that cloud Lorraine detached a mass of the Swiss to follow round secretly by the hollow lane along the woodside. So they came up, unperceived, upon the flank of the Burgundians.

But those Burgundians, Charles's men, stood in rank awaiting the shock upon their front, ignorant of the turning column. They were but five thousand all told, and against them were two men to their one. They knew not that half their enemies had thus been detached secretly to the west. Still they waited, confident in the strength of their position: waiting for the heavy armed knights of Lorraine to charge.

Even as they so stood, the Burgundians heard something which no troops will stand—the sound of attack behind their line.

It was the custom of the Swiss to sound their horns three times just before they struck, and that loud, unexpected challenge came where none thought soldiers to be—far off and behind them to their right, from the woodside.

It was in vain that Charles attempted to convert his line to the right, to face that sudden danger; it was in vain that he called for the guns to be dragged round and faced westward to the wood and the Swiss. All came too late; for all was in confusion, and already his line was dissolving. Upon such a beginning of chaos Lorraine, from the front, charged; and with that the Burgundian troops became a mob, and the action, hardly begun, turned at once into a slaughter.

Charles's cavalry, upon the left, near the river, cut itself out across the water, losing heavily, the horses stamping through the thin ice, and a remnant escaping by that ford.

Round the great Duke himself a devoted centre rallied, half of them of his nobility, but it could not stand—it was forced back in the general flood, and all the two miles of ground that afternoon (the snow had ceased, and the sun shone upon the carnage) was filled with a confused mass of massacre and of flight. The Swiss and the Germans and the French lords of the Barrois pressed on into the midst of the broken herd, right up to the walls of the town.

A mile from the city gate there ran a brook, the brook of St. John. There, in the hurly-burly, Charles the Bold, Duke of Burgundy, parried right and left desperately, his lords about him, and in their midst were the enemy, ahorse and afoot, the long halberds of the Swiss, thrusting pikes, and the swing of swords.

None knew the great Duke Charles in such a confusion. They saw his rich armour, but they had no other sign; for the golden lion of Burgundy upon his helm had fallen even before the battle, and he himself, as he saw the crest tumble on his saddle bow, all those hours before, had muttered: "An omen—*signum dei!*"

So that man, unknown to the enemy, fought hard with his visor down. A thrust took him in the left thigh, another in the back. As he reeled he cried "Bourgoyne!" but one Claude, the Lord of Bauzemont, who was fighting there for Lorraine, hearing that cry, thrust a lance at him, not knowing whom he struck. The helm and its visor shattered. The face of the great Duke was gashed from ear to chin, and he went down. None knew who had so fallen, for all the nobles about him also were destroyed. And that was the end of Charles the Bold.

*   *   *   *   *

The press of the conquerors rushed up to the city gate, the Gate of St. Nicholas. The starving people ran to cheer, the garrison let down the bridge beyond the town, the last remnants of Charles's force were massacred at the bridge of Bouxières.

The wintry sun was setting. The force had its hold again upon all the fields. The Duke of Lorraine held festival that night—back in his own city, and all his people eating again and drinking, and rejoicing in victory.

But one thing checked his triumph: whither had Charles gone? Was he in Metz, or fled perhaps into the Germanies, or got home among his own people in the Low Countries?

All the next day, Twelfth Day, the Feast of the Kings, they searched the battlefield, heaps of naked bodies stripped by the spoilers, but none could say that they had found the great Duke. But that evening, as Lorraine rode back into Nancy, despondent and fearful, a captain brought to him a young page, one of the Colonnas of

Rome, and said to him: "This lad knew the great Duke."

So next morning, the Tuesday, the 7th of January, very early, they went out among the bodies in the snow, and the Italian boy would say first of one, then of another: "It is not he . . . it is not he." And with him also went one who had been a maid in the service of Charles. Then, at last, they came to the strong body, lying all wounds, with its dreadful gashed face, and the mass of thick, black hair against the snow, and the Italian page cried, "That is the Duke," and the servant knelt down crying and sobbing, and they heard her say, "Ha! Burgundy, my Lord! my Lord!"

René of Lorraine had that famous body lifted with reverence, and wrapped in a linen shroud, and carried with pomp into Nancy.

*   *   *   *   *

Thenceforward, with whatever vicissitude of come and go, the Rhine was recovered for the Gauls.

TWO SATURDAYS

(Montmartre and Amboise)

(August 15, 1534; *March* 16, 1560)

TWO scenes, half a lifetime apart, small, detailed, vivid, mark the enormous storm of the Reformation in the Gauls—that vast battle which was never wholly won or lost, no, not to this day; for France is the arena of Europe. Each of these little scenes was an origin: the one of the force that half-reconquered Europe for the Church, the Jesuits; the other of the force that, taking arms for Calvinism, all but conquered the crown—the force of the great nobles in rebellion, of the gentry, of the merchants in their towns, and of the peasants in the central hills, the Huguenots.

*   *   *   *   *

In the morning of Saturday, August the 15th, in the year 1534, the Feast of the Assumption, six men of various age came to the little room on the hill of the university, where lived, determined, eager, somewhat silent, a dark, square-headed Basque, whose military temper was to half change the world. An intense devotion, a burning life within, an absorption in divine things and in the fate of the soul, made this man single from all of his fellows. None met him but went away with an impression as of flame. It was Ignatius of Loyola in his forty-fourth year.

The six who thus came together up the stone stairs to that little room, with its crucifix, its narrow bed, its bare table, its empty walls, were all men who had come under that profound influence; men of the university, like himself—men already filled with the conception of a mission. There, leading them, was yet another Basque, called from his mother's name Xavier, six years younger than the chief. There was young Salman of Toledo, a boy of nineteen; there was Laynez the Castilian, just of age; Alphonso of Valladolid; Rodriguez of Portugal; and (the only Gaul among them) a peasant from the hills of Savoy, long plunged into the study of the academies, not yet thirty: Faber, from the hamlet, and the Alpine huts of Villaret. He alone was a priest.

When they were thus assembled they set out about their purpose.

They went them down the university hill by that straight and narrow Roman street which crosses Paris from south to north, and is here the street of St. James, there of St. Martin. They traversed the twin bridges of the island, they went the full mile to the city wall, passed through St. Martin's Gate, and, outside, were in the fields. The hill of Montmartre stood before them, its gypsum quarries, its crazy windmills, and on the summit a little old church—poor, for it had few parishioners. It was called Our Lady of the Martyrs, and thither were they bound upon this, Her feast day.

They climbed the hill. They went down by the little stair near the porch, which leads into the crypt of that strange place, and where the stones go back to the temple of the pagan days. Faber vested and began the Mass.

When he came to the Communion, the six laymen rose and knelt at the altar rails. Then, one by one in order each, before receiving the Host, took in a loud voice the vow of their companionship, and Faber himself, the last, pronounced those words. The Ablutions were received. The post-Communions read, the last Gospel recited. The Society of Jesus was founded.

* * * * *

The winter was not over in Blois—the winter

of 1560. The old king, who had so sternly maintained the national religion, was dead; a boy of fifteen reigned—frail, incompetent, diseased—the son of that Medicean woman whom an enemy has called "the worm from the tomb of Italy."

The child was married to a child-wife, the daughter of the King of Scotland, Mary Stuart. It was she, in part, already masterful, that had called to that Court her mother's brothers, the sons of Lorraine, the Guises; grandsons of that same man who had entered his capital of Nancy on the death of Charles the Bold.

And they were hated. They were not of the national nobility; they had enriched themselves scandalously. If they were to be the protectors of the Church, it was but another weakness for the Church. One of their group, a child of fourteen, had been made Archbishop of Rheims, and loaded with the wealth of such great names as Cluny—St. Bernard's glorious house; as Marmoutier—St. Martin's immemorial foundation. Scandal! Scandal!

Against these men, against the new, feeble, immature king, rose muttering throughout the commonwealth all forms of opposition, linked under the bond (here loose, there strict) of the Reform, of the Gospellers, of them that would be rid of their fathers, and who were clamped to the iron of Calvin. He, far off in Geneva, commanded. Already, some few months since, the Reformers had organized everywhere. They had held their first synod, making them one thing throughout the territory of France, and, by hundreds, the armed gentry were rallying, though secretly, to that standard. Men from all countries leaked in to take service in the coming war as mercenaries. Many from the Germanies, many from Switzerland. They were sworn in secrecy by the German freebooters' oath: "To follow the dumb captain." And of the native people crowds were ready, when the signal should be given, to join the nobles who were moving. By little groups, and as single men, they came filtering through towards the Loire.

What could the Guises bring against that? There were no armies in those days, save such guards as the king could pay, or such gentry as would still obey his summons.

The plot was laid to seize the crowned boy while the Court thus still sat in Blois, for the town was open and without walls. A mob could carry it. The leaders still professed that to this boy they wished no harm. It was his counsellors they would be rid of, and all their hatred was

for the Guises—especially for the duke, their
head, the real ruler.

But before the appointed day the young king,
restless, must be moving down river. He would
hunt, and he was tired of the woods to the west
and to the south. The Court set out. It was
through this chance whim that the rising was
postponed and lost its vigour. It was through
this chance whim that the threatened Court
found itself safe in the little stronghold of
Amboise.

As it there sat it felt in the air a menace all
around. They had summoned and held hostage
in the castle one or two of the greatest among
those whom they knew to be their secret enemies.
But the populace also was astir. Not all looks
were kind, and there were strange men on market
days.

Some order misunderstood, some rashness, pro-
voked a misfire. A crowd of men made for the
castle, not all of them unarmed, professing that
they must see the king. They were rejected; con-
temptuously enough young Francis II. even scattered coins among them, as being of the poor and
common people. That was only the grumbling
of something distant.

It was on Saturday, the 16th of March, that

the storm broke; but even then, ill-led. Men came swarming out from the woods on the south of the town. It was an armed attack. It has been called "The Tumult of Amboise." The leaders were few, ill-chosen and worse followed. Not enough of the gentry were there. Horsemen and armour were lacking. It could but fail. The gates were shut in time, the ramparts armed, the wave of attack broke against impregnable walls; it was shot down under the trained aim of the archers; it was pursued, dispersed, driven to its woods again, and, on the way, whole dozens were rounded up and bound, and beaten, and thrust back into the castle as prisoners. For days the hanging of them went on, from the gibbet of the town itself, from the beams of the main gateway of the castle, from the iron crooks on its walls.

The thing was over, and it had seemed small. The young queen had laughed at it. But it was the beginning of that tremendous business which was to fill all France with death and the destruction of lovely stone; to sow a permanent division, to leave, much later, the Bourbons supreme, and not even to end when the thirteenth Louis should have ridden out to strike the last blow at La Rochelle—how many years to come!

THE FRONTIER

(*September* 9, 1642)

RICHELIEU, the Cardinal, was growing old, his work was nearly accomplished. It was the recovery of the frontiers, and on the south those limits were the Pyrenees.

The long process of the hotch-potch of popular movement and feeling over fifteen hundred years had blurred the outline of Gaul. It was his business to restore an exact shape and a true wall to the inheritance of the kings—"The Square Field."

To the east the thing had never been possible, and perhaps never will be. The Rhine stood clearly before all eyes. The Rhine could be reached, but never made a final decision. Reached, it must be crossed; but reached at one point it could not be reached in all. There would ever be a struggle in those march lands. It is a struggle woefully present to us to-day. Elsewhere the sea, the Alps, made definite boundaries. There remained the Pyrenees.

But until this time the Pyrenees had not been attained. The tide of Gallic power had overflowed them, and again had ebbed; and those confused and noble valleys held races which overspread the crest, and none of which had felt themselves at heart to be either of the northern or of the southern land; neither of the pastures and the rivers and the woods of Gascony, nor of the hard and burnt Iberian rock and dust. Richelieu desired that crest and those limits, and that long mountain boundary against the sky.

Where that singular straight line of division, the most unbroken wall in Europe, reaches the Mediterranean, the Catalonian people and their language held all the passes and spread to the north and to the south, one nation—or at least one race. These, so early as Charlemagne, had been the march of the Ebro, and Barcelona, the great port, had remained the capital of one countryside. But in the darkness after the death of Charlemagne no man could tell you whether its fate would fall to the north or to the south. It acquired an independence which at first was feudal, and might later well have been national, as that of Portugal became, as that which little Andorra still holds in its fantastic isolated cup. Through the Middle Ages the thing had swung now to the French, now to the Spaniards, but still was Catalan: one thing. The genius of Richelieu, to the disadvantage of that entity, to the advantage of his sovereign, was to divide it by the crest of the Pyrenees, and to push the writ of Paris up to that sombre line where the peaks go down in lessening but rugged summits, and lose themselves in the salt—diminishing to mere rocks at last. For Richelieu had determined, not that all the Catalonian land, but only this province—this northern province of it, the Roussillon, hither of the Pyrenees—should be French; the rest he would leave to Spain.

He played for the furtherance of this end upon a spirit which he flattered and nourished, but did not fulfil—the spirit of Catalan independence.

The great Spanish monarchy, almost the master of the world, had, in the century before, firmly established itself over the whole Peninsula, suppressing local liberties, centralizing, despotic. Against that awful monarchy, against its symbol, the angry Catalans had risen; and, supporting that rising in the enormous duel between the house of Spain and the house of France, Richelieu had permitted the rebels to elect his master their Count.

On January 23, 1641, following upon treaties of alliance between the Catalan rebels and the French Crown, Louis XIII. was admitted Count of Barcelona, monarch of all that country on either side of the hills. But the game which Richelieu played had not Barcelona for its stakes; he was gambling for the Roussillon only, and for Perpignan.

All the strength of Castille, all the men Spain could spare from the universal war, were poured into the defence of Perpignan, and La Rena was sent as governor to hold that northern bastion, and prevent the French advance to the Pyrenees.

The town lies sloping downwards westward from its citadel. It stands in a sheet of vine-yards; a plain having to the east, solemnly domi-nating it, all the huge mass of the Canigou. La Rena held it strongly. He would quarter his soldiers upon the townsmen. They resisted. He turned his guns from the citadel upon the burgh-ers, and they surrendered, but not before nearly six hundred of their houses had been ruined by the fire. They had attempted a truce; the bishop had gone up to the citadel with the Sacrament in a procession. They obtained no truce; goods were looted, gallows were raised in the market-place, and Olivares, the great minister of the Spanish king, was supreme.

So Perpignan was held in that summer of 1641 for Spain.

The plain around was flooded with the French. South, north, east, west of the city their eight thousand infantry, their two regiments of cavalry, garrisoned the villages and towns, until at last, by the end of the year, Perpignan itself was blockaded, and before any siege lines were formed a famine had begun. In that winter, in the January of 1642, the struggle opened between the two powers. Brézé, coming to Catalonia as the Viceroy of Louis XIII., sat down before Perpignan; but he could not quite cut off relief—some wheat got in before the end of the month. From Castille no further troops could come in relief. Still the French flooded on, La Meilleraye at their head; and with him, second in command, a name that was to be more than famous—Turenne.

By April the last of the small desperate Spanish garrisons in the neighbourhood of Collioure had surrendered, but Perpignan still held.

All France seemed to be pressing on to that one point. The Cardinal himself took the long journey, fell ill, and stopped at Narbonne. His master, the king, Louis XIII., went forward, and on the 23rd May took up his station in the farm which used to be called the Mas of John Pauques, which is still known to-day as the King's Farm; near St. Stevens, looking upon the city.

By this time all Europe looked on.

The cavalry of the guard was there: Enghien, Polignac, Cinq-Mars, Schomberg—all the great names; and the musketeers of the Cardinal were there as well. Nearly thirty thousand men stood thus before the walls, which had become the test of whether the government of Paris should or should not come up to the Pyrenees.

Behind those walls, unsuccoured, the last veterans of the Thirty Years' War—not three thousand of them, and of these but a nucleus Castillian —still held. They were the men whom all Europe had learnt to regard as masters, but the odds were too great. They could stand one to ten, even famished, behind a formidable trench and wall, but as they stood they died of the fever and of the famine.

As the heat grew, and as the grapes began to show their first clusters in the great sweep of vineyards under that mound which watched the drama from the west, the two captains, Avila and Cavabro, refused to treat. The citizens had been made their slaves. The citadel was their vantage ground, and from it a ceaseless pillage ruined the town. If ever the moral force of civilians counts in war, it was here accumulated against the fierce and terrible captains of Castille, as strong as iron in pride, but now doomed.

Every animal in the place was eaten. The citizens were thrown back upon the rooks and the rats; the wounded in the hospital ate the straw of their beds, and men were seen in the streets of the city gathering the weeds of the wayside.

The captains of Philip IV. still held.

He made a desperate effort at relief. He drove the French from Barcelona; but he could not find more men, harassed as he was all over Europe, for that one essential point of Perpignan. A little body came up under Torrecusa; La Mothe-Houdancourt held it off beyond the hills.

It was the height of summer, and under the burning sun the ill fortune of the Spanish star saw to it that, as a last resort, a fleet attempting a diversion by the coast should have a tempest raised against it and should fly to the Balearics.

Then it was at last that Avila despaired. But even then he could not sign a capitulation. He signed only a document by which he pledged himself to surrender if no help should come before a date which was discussed by the starving men and fixed at last upon the 9th of September. The 9th of September came; no succour had arrived. The gates were opened, the keys delivered, and the play was done.

The Castillians had demanded and obtained the honours of war. The French in two ranks saw passing between them the haggard remnant of all this heroism, still attempting some severity of demeanour. A generous instinct had moved the French command to see that none of the Catalans, none of the town folk in their hatred of the Spanish garrison, should be seen. It was the northern soldiers of Louis XIII. who held them back as the tiny garrison marched out, concealing its weakness under a mask of order and of discipline.

Their officers saluted the French flag, and at their head Avila rode one of the last horses. The ceremony was over; the Castillians, not prisoners, were outside the lines.

Avila dismounted, knelt upon the ground, looked south towards Spain and to the arms of Spain upon the gate. His eyes were full of tears. As he knelt he raised his right hand towards the town, and made a great sign of the Cross against the sky, so bidding it farewell for ever.

It was by the Canet Gate that these few heroes went forth after the last effort for their king. It was by the Gate of Elne that there marched in at the same moment the fresh, the well-fed, strong-bodied northern Frenchmen, six thousand strong, and behind them an immense train of wagons, filled with wheat, barley, oats, bread ready-baked, bacon and fresh meat—food for a year.

In the Cathedral of St. John the Archbishop of Narbonne and the Bishops of Nîmes and Albi, crowded around by the enthusiastic men of the Catalans, sang the Te Deum. But far off in the Escorial, Olivares, having heard the news, leant for the moment against the stone wall, and the palm of his left hand pressed upon it, and then moved towards the little room where the king was still reading and signing his papers.

He fell upon his knees and wept, and said that it was time that he, Olivares, should, by his own wish, die; and even so, he dared not say the words that would give the reason of his despair. He waited until his master spoke and asked him what so moved him.

"Sire," said that strong man, sobbing, and still upon his knees, "you have lost Perpignan!"

Then Philip answered in a low voice, but gravely: "We must submit to the will of God."

THE EXILE

(*December* 30, 1688)

THERE are many squares of soil where the histories of nations touch and the fate of the one is intermixed with the fate of the other upon a few roods of land.

There are the battlefields, of course—but that is obvious. There are the conference rooms: the rooms in which treaties were signed; though most treaties do not mean very much to history, some are of prodigious effect—witness the Treaty of the Pyrenees. There are the universally sacred sites—like the pavement of St. Peter's, old and new. There are the sites of Decisions, like the quays of Calais; like the palaces of Vienna—where the agents of Governments have met and have doubtfully decided, for a little time, the inferior interests of men—the mechanical interests of men.

But there are also less known places where the fates of nations met oddly, sharply, sometimes fruitfully, sometimes unfruitfully.

For instance, just outside Montreuil, two coaches passed each other in the night—the one going north, the other going south. The one going south was that of the British envoy prepared for war with the French Republic in 1793; the one going north was that bearing the French envoy with orders to prevent war if possibly that could be done.

Of those squares of land, one is not as famous as it should be. It is the land upon which stands the seventeenth-century palace of St. Germains, with the terrace just outside overlooking the plain of the Seine and the low grey line of Paris far beyond, and the distant, diminished towers of St. Denis.

Had the Stuarts returned to the throne of England, that place would be famous enough. It would be counted as the point of their departure, as the rallying place of their cause, as the seed of a new time. It would be a place of national pilgrimage and sacred in English eyes; for there it was that James II., the rightful English king, came as an exile to meet his cousin of France. But the Stuarts did not return; and, therefore, the incident has been pushed away into the lumber-room. There is thought to be something futile about St. Germains. Even Culloden is more famous.

Yet St. Germains has good material for a

shrine. It remains just what it was. The past lives there. It is what it is, although success did not follow on the meeting it saw. It is precisely what it would have been had success followed that meeting. It is still itself. I could wish that the tragedy of that palace were better known.

Mary of Modena had come over hurriedly with the child, the heir to the English throne. She had been housed in this palace by the gratitude, the courtesy, and the high policy of Louis XIV., King of France. She was the Queen of England, and the usurpers were (officially) of no account to Versailles. The fatigue of the journey, of the alarms, of the perils, had oppressed the young woman; she had taken to her bed. In a fine cradle, worthy of royalty, swinging in the same room, lay that little baby who was later to be James III., and never to reign.

Louis XIV. had returned to visit this lady; he had come to her bedside again, making obeisance and reverence, as king to queen. They awaited James himself, for they knew that if he could escape the plots of his enemies he would reach them. The news had come of his landing. He had reached port in the dead of the Christmas dark, at three in the morning. He had travelled down from the sea-coast with haste. He came in no very great state to the doors of that palace, late upon this December (for the French this January) day. The weather was stormy; he had had no relief from travel; his great boots were splashed with mud, and the tails of his long coat also; and his odd, energetic, somewhat pinched face showed his fatigue. Yet he was the King of England, and kingship was the high political note of the time. He was the son of Henrietta Maria, consort of Charles I. No one had a moment's right against himself—least of all his disappointed, soured, usurping daughter; his alien, vicious, usurping son-in-law.

The man who had had, in varying proportions, ill-fortune to oppress him, ill-judgment to urge him on (but much more ill-fortune than ill-judgment), this courageous, intelligent, tenacious, but now defeated man, stepped down unaided, but awkwardly, from the coach. He was cramped by his journey.

Notice had been given to Louis XIV., sitting there by the bedside in the room above; and that great king, holding the highest throne in Europe, came down at once, almost eagerly, almost forgetting the ritual of his position, to honour such an occasion and such an exile.

The rain still fell slantwise in the open court-yard of that palace of brick and cornered stone. Louis XIV., in plumed hat, and cloak, and sword, and buckled shoes, walked through the weather, indifferent, his gentlemen about him—walked, I say, even eagerly, with some forgetfulness of what he owed to his own royalty, so sharply did he feel the strength of the occasion.

They met under the arch of the portcullis where the guard were mounted, on the house side of the drawbridge, and in that meeting there was something consonant to the ideas of their time, grotesque to those of ours. For you must know that the men of that time bowed low to their superiors—lower and lower in proportion, not to their own inferiority, but to the greatness of him whom they saluted. Now, here were two equals —the King of England and the King of France— meeting to salute the one the other; so each bowed lower and lower as they approached, each sweeping his hat in his hand before him, and modulating his steps exactly as the ritual of that time demanded: the left foot advanced, then the right at right angles to it, in something more like a dance than a walk.

With all this they must give each other the

accolade: they were equals; they must embrace as equals. So the arms of the one man, bowed down and obeisant with his head (a large wig upon it), were spread out, inviting, upon either side of his body, the right hand holding the large plumed hat, the left hand making gestures with its fingers in the air.

At last, in such a progress, the two bodies must meet; and so they did. The reception of the one to the other was what we, to-day, mocking such things, might compare to the beginning of a wrestling match. But the onlookers had no such profanity in their minds. For them (and they were right) this strange ceremony was a high symbol. The Great King was treating the ruined Exile as an equal, and some future might be built upon such a foundation. The Stuarts might yet return. For that meeting—to us, as we call up its physical details, grotesque; to them, sublime —might well have been the beginning of a true Restoration, and of an England happier and better than she has been—perhaps less wealthy.

It was not so to be. The ceremony was sterile. It bred no issue. There was to come the Boyne, the 'Fifteen, the 'Forty-five—and nothingness; at last a grave in Rome, and that small, noble memorial in St. Peter's, which I, for my part, never pass without a movement of the heart. The Stuarts were not to return.

*   *   *   *   *

Next day the great king came back to his exiles at St. Germains, and later in the week he came once more. Each time he visited them with an increasing sincerity and fervour of support. He leaned long over the cradle and gazed down at the little Heir of England, with more feeling than he had been known to show in looking at any of his own children.

But, high above men, the fates had decided and the stars were set. For business of this sort works out very slowly; and not within the lives of two or three men that meet, but in many generations, are the ultimate purposes accomplished; and though the Stuarts did not return, perhaps they are to watch their revenge.

THE MONEY-LENDER

(*May* 6, 1708)

A FINE day in May, and the spring had been early that year. The trees were well out. A soft wind under a benignant sun came up from the valley of the Seine, through the woods, and blessed the formal new greatness of Marly; the splendour and melancholy of the great water-basins, the majesty of the walls, were still new. The trees had not yet that height which adds nobility to the noble lines of the place. But already there was upon it the stamp of so great a reign. Largeness and order and perfection of proportion were everywhere.

The palace stood alone, its dependencies grouped about it with a space between. The front court and approach were deserted; but in the grounds behind groups had formed: knots of courtiers were discussing some coming thing, and all the life of the monarchy was disturbed in that fine spring leisure, both in the great rooms of the palace and in the gardens.

Twelve pavilions or lodges stood in formal order round behind the main building, the lawns between. They were habitations for men and women favoured of the king. Before one of these stood a man whose long acquaintance with affairs on the one hand, with the Court upon the other, had not quite rid him of awkwardness; for he remembered his humble birth. It was Desmarets, the Controller of Finance, a man of fifty. By his side, of equal age, stood, simply dressed, demure, but a little sullen, a stout figure, odd in such surroundings—Bernard the Jew. One or two others talked to him, some commonplaces or other, as they thus stood before the pavilion. It looked like a chance group; yet it was designed. And why it was designed one must go back some weeks, some months, to understand.

* * * * *

Desmarets, coming back to the control of Louis XIV.'s finance in the winter before that spring, in the February, knew not which way to turn for monies in the conduct of the war. He bethought him of one who had become the richest man in Europe—Bernard the Banker.

He knew his task to be difficult: the credit of the king was bad, the war was a bottomless pit, swallowing million after million, the security of the taxes was exhausted; he also knew Bernard by repute: that repute was not in favour of the task.

Bernard was a man notoriously cold in judgment—and notoriously right. So it was that he had built up his immense wealth. He had been born the son of an artist, an etcher and engraver, indifferent to anything but his art. He had been born the son of one of those Jewish men of talent, whose every mark it is to concentrate wholly upon the business of their lives, without concern for wealth, or even (very much) for fame. From such a beginning, young in such surroundings, Samuel Bernard the younger had re-acted toward a patient accumulation of gold. His art, his task, had been that. Amply had he succeeded; but when Desmarets approached him in the desperate crisis of that year, not a gold piece was forthcoming.

In those days men were free, and the rulers of a state could not ruin them for a whim—even a whim of war. How, then, was Bernard to be persuaded?

Desmarets had seen the king, and what followed here at Marly was the fruit of what the king had heard.

Desmarets had told the king that not a gold piece was forthcoming.

Bernard was hard as a rock. He had wasted no time in courtesy. He had not even wasted time on insult; he had not sneered with the sneer that is common to such occasions. He had said, simply and briefly enough, that there was no security. Where might not such a beginning lead? The money would be poured out like water upon sand. The war was interminable, and the people could bear no more taxes. In our time a man like Desmarets could have threatened. In that time he could not threaten, but he bethought himself of something else, and it was upon this something else that he had spoken to the king.

Hence it was, these few months after, in the opening of the spring, in the May following that February, that he, Desmarets, and Bernard, happened to be standing near the pavilion at the back of the palace of Marly. Bernard sullen, as I have said, and wondering why he had been asked here to no purpose; Desmarets affecting indifference and leisure, but inwardly on thorns.

Just as this waiting of theirs was getting too awkward (Desmarets wondering how much longer it would last, Bernard wondering what it was all about, and almost proposing to go) there appeared, sauntering towards them with dignity

and at leisure, speaking in low tones to the couple
that were with him (and who showed an exaggerated deference in their demeanour), a man of
singular appearance.

It was the king.

He was seventy years of age. His years
showed, not in his gait (for that had always been
leisurely and dignified), nor in his carriage, for
his pride kept him upright to the end; nor even in
his body, dressed as it was for his part. He had
a double chin, but not exaggerated; the strong,
continuous line of his arched nose and high fore-
head showed now in profile even more than they
had done in his youth; his mouth was firm; his
eyes, though veiled with age, were still vigorous.
Where you saw the approach of his end was in
the fatigue of the face at its sides—the many
wrinkles at the corners of the eyes, the weaken-
ing flesh of the cheeks, and the slight droop at
the corners of the lips. But a man accustomed
throughout a lifetime to full command, and commanding with vigour and with judgment, he
remained to the end inspired by such a spiritual
posture. He was about to demean himself spirit-
ually very much indeed, but the garments, the
exteriors of dignity, he never lost.

When he had come within a few yards of

Desmarets and of Bernard, he looked up as though surprised to see them, while they uncovered and bowed.

"Why, Desmarets," said he, "whom have you here?"

"It is Mr. Samuel Bernard."

"I thought as much. . . . Mr. Bernard," Louis added, as though it were a sudden thought and a pleasant one, "I wonder if you have ever looked round my gardens here at Marly?"

The king's companions stepped back somewhat, and left him alone with those other two. Bernard replied with an awed mumble. . . . His whole being was filled with the greatness of the occasion.

It was one thing to be proud of his money and to found himself upon it solidly in his office with some fellow or other who had risen to the control of the finance, and who might be called Desmarets. It was another to be in the presence of Louis XIV. He felt himself a little weak at the knees, and yet happy to be in a new heavenly world. He bowed awkwardly again at the wrong time, and once again he mumbled.

"Why," said the old king, with a false sprightliness and affected gaiety, "you *must* see my gardens. . . . Come with me. . . . Desmarets," he added, turning to that courtier with an assumed ease, "I will not deprive you long of Mr. Bernard's company; I am sure you will be eager to have him back. I only want to show him the gardens."

Desmarets bowed again in a trained manner, Bernard awkwardly; and the king took Bernard off to see the gardens: a nice little way-mark in the social history of Europe!

One companion the king kept with him as a sort of foil, for with Bernard alone he would have felt like a man alone with a monster. Louis dared not trust himself with Bernard alone, therefore did he keep that one companion as a foil. But the companion was to remain silent while Louis did the honours.

"Are not they well chosen, these chestnuts? Not one has failed! . . . They are young yet, Mr. Bernard. *You* will see them grow tall. . . . But I am an old man. . . . Their alignment is perfect."

Bernard said in a husky voice, forcing himself to speak, "All these hills are market-garden country. The soil is good. The best trees are nourished here. . . ." Then he added, "Sire," and gulped.

The king approved his judgment.

"You are right, Mr. Bernard," he said, trying to be as little pompous as he could. "You are curiously right. . . . It is a most interesting view." He then added (lying), "Few have remarked this. It is most interesting that you should have remarked it. We have here at Marly an excellent soil for the rapid growth of great trees. Now I see there a poplar: we have also poplars . . . but their arrangement seems to me a little spoilt by the cross paths. There is something irregular about the genius of these trees. I should have had them set farther back, as with a hint of forestry."

Saying this, the king halted, leaned back, gazed at the unoffending poplars with severity, then turned, looked at Bernard, and smiled painfully.

"Your Majesty is right," said Bernard. "You are right . . ." (correcting himself), "Sire."

The banker had not meant the phrase to be blunt, yet Louis restrained himself like a man who feels a sudden pain; then he continued rapidly, and as though to forget what had just passed,—

"You have studied gardens, Mr. Bernard?" (Without waiting for an answer) "They are the most charming of studies. They never grow stale. There is a book I must show you" (he shuddered

inwardly as he said it), "the plans of which perpetually please me, thought they are only plans.
I conjure up gardens as I look at them. One is
at Tarbles. . . . I shall never see it" (a little
sadly), "but I almost seem to know it from the
plans."

Bernard answered, "One must always see the
plan first," and there was silence for a full sixty
seconds as they continued that mortal progress.
But Bernard already trod on air for all his bulk
and for all his furious shyness in such company.

The king, without glancing sideways (which
would have been an unkingly thing to do),
gauged in his mind the distance between the place
which they had reached and the point to which
they must return. He decided to suggest the
return.

Now when the king would suggest a change
of direction from one path to another, those of
the Court needed no direction. Their eyes were
upon the master, who was also the nation, and,
for that matter, the summit of Europe; and while
they said this or that, in the careful wit of their
time, they saw exactly which way the royal hands
waved, and which way the royal feet were
turning.

Not so Bernard; he had not the habit. Therefore, when the steps of Louis turned to the right, to go back towards the pavilion by the farther path, the banker almost stumbled into the king.

Louis, with perfect restraint, half halted for a moment. Bernard recovered himself and murmured an apology of the middle classes. The king was too well-bred even to hear it, and the retreat upon Marly began.

There was no awkwardness. The same fatuous phrases—or if not fatuous, only not fatuous because there was tradition behind the whole affair—proceeded one after the other from the lips of France; the same rare, uncertain agreement, increasingly filled with awe, came, murmured rather than spoken, from the lips of Bernard.

He was returned to Desmarets. The goods were delivered.

It had been a wonderful quarter of an hour for Bernard! The king had shewn him Marly! He could say all his life, and his children could say to their children, "The king himself took me all round his gardens at Marly!" To tell the full truth, he hardly knew what he had seen. He remembered six young chestnuts and a mist of poplars, and he had been conscious of a Presence always there upon his left, and that he was making history.

Already Bernard was a different man. The king, lingering just enough to make the parting easy, moved off, erect, and, as it would have seemed to a very acute observer, a little less restrained. A very acute observer would have noted in the gesture of his arms and in the carriage of his body, as Louis moved off, something of relief. But only a very acute observer could have noticed this. It was the slightest of slight changes.

Meanwhile Bernard, left behind, had become voluble. He began to talk at large upon Marly, upon the glories of the gardens. He bored Desmarets most damnably, but Desmarets affected an equal eagerness, pretended surprise, put on a familiar astonishment at each new detail, and with slow, familiar steps took Bernard back to his sumptuous carriage at the gates. He held his smile well back as the banker was helped into the cushions by absurdly obsequious servants. He saw the splendid four horses stamp off down the big cobblestones of the yard.

The man gone, Desmarets sat himself down frankly, without ceremony, upon a bench, as though to rest from a great strain. A courtier came up to him. He did not rise. The courtier said,—

"That's all over!"

But Desmarets answered,—

"There is much more in Bernard than one might think. . . . I like him." Which was a lie.

And a very few days later the Crown began its drain of nine millions upon Bernard.

THE CHÂTEAU

(*October* 1759)

THERE is a great house which stood once in the woods of a small village some three miles from Versailles. It still stands, and woods about it. I know it well.

It is built in the majestic and sober manner of its time—not quite two hundred years ago; airy, in great suites of rooms, with the windows lighting them from either side. The ground falls away from before it in a park with tall trees forming a sweep of descending lawn, and is faced by the enclosing hills, where the trees hide all but the summit of a long, arched aqueduct, which furnished the fountains of the king's palace. The west illumines that slope at evening; the summer sun sets behind the arches of that old, high aqueduct on its ridges of the hills, and far away beyond, miles away, are the farther hills, which are the threshold of the Vexin; while to the right, to the northwards, lies mistedly the plain of the Seine. In this house, in the very heart of the eighteenth century, and in the crisis of its fate, Louis, the king of France, the fifteenth of that name, sat waiting by the fire; for it was autumn, and they had brought in chestnut logs from the woods and lit them.

The coach stood outside the glass-roofed porch, having just brought its master—for he had come suddenly, capriciously, without warning, as was his habit in these last years—and the Pompadour was within.

He sat there waiting for her, putting out his hands in a simple gesture towards the fire, unwatched, alone; his fine deep eyes were full of mood and reverie, and also of the beginnings of despair; but he had come for companionship.

The brief two years of passion, the three years of intimacy, had passed, but something more enduring remained in that strange soul which could not tear itself away from any roots, and yet could not act: full of energy within, of emotion, even of desire; but lacking the strength to pierce that shell which cursedly fenced it from the outside world. There he sat, waiting for the Pompadour, and still putting out his hands to the warmth of the fire after the damp coldness of that autumn drive.

In the vestibule without, four gentlemen whispered; and in the far staircases of the place a discreet servant had brought the message to his friend.

Before that fire, less lonely for his loneliness, the last of the undisturbed kings, the last secure king of that tremendous line, communed with his own mind.

It was not a communion of despair, though despair was creeping in to the outer parts of his soul; it was a communion of hopeless fatigue—not fatigue as yet of the body, but an impossible fatigue of the soul; his body was still strong; his soul could still perfectly use that instrument—yet there was nothing left; he had tried all things. He had discovered in childhood how this half-divine position cut him off from men. He had hated, he had accepted, he had used his isolation; he had tried to be two men—and the end of that is destruction. He had tried to be what all his duty should make him, and yet to be a man surrounded by habits and by a domestic air. Under the twin effort he had fallen to be a man entirely alone, yet with certain friends; yet with one friend—no longer a lover, but notedly a friend.

The restlessness which came of his unhappy mood stirred him as he thus sat alone. He swung up suddenly from his chair, turned round, peered here and there at ornaments in the room before him, looked closely at a piece of Chinese work upon a shelf, thought it odd, yet discovered at once its genius; then strolled to the long window upon his right, and looked with eyes too full of reminiscence towards the aqueduct and the wooded hill. The autumn evening was reddening, but there was sun behind the clouds, and, far on the horizon, a shaft of light against which St. Germains stood delicately. . . . All his life had run in that little groove of one countryside—the Parisis. He had lost power to feel other things, and yet he remembered one or two longer drives, and he smiled as he thought of the noise, the peril, the wind, the acclamations of Fontenoy, and the repose of that battle-evening after victory.

It was more than four years gone; he was in the fifth year from that great day. But five years seems long in what is still the active middle of life. Too soon was he to know how five years would race by in the degradation of sense, when the later years of a man have led him into a closed labyrinth of lust.

As he still stood looking to the north through the window across that afternoon autumn air, with the majesty of the high trees framing his landscape, he heard a step he thought he knew. His attitude changed. He started round. It died away again. She was long in coming!

He felt the chill of his place, and, sensitive to every slight impression of the body, long steeped in immediate enjoyment of every detail of luxury, he moved at once instinctively back to that chair before the fire and sat him down again; but this time leaning backwards, his arms on the arms of the gilded thing that supported him, and a deeper reverie in his eyes.

The chestnut logs had caught; they made a murmuring which effaced time and were a sort of lullaby. For some few moments he did not know that he was waiting for a step and a voice, though they were those of a friend. For some few moments he did but dream, and there passed before his mind certain odd convictions which inhabited it, and certain common terrors; both of these stood against a background of disappointment and of nothingness. . . . None of his line could be lost . . . none of his line could be lost. . . . St. Louis had baptized them all into a sort of security. . . . If only the poor were not oppressed, if only he were always master of the rich, and a true king, his soul would be at last secure. . . . Nor was he too much to blame. These awful and remote dignities of kingship must be counterweighted by something human; it was a crying need; and affection, though passing, was still affection. . . . There was no gallery of faces in his mind . . . he had been good to all these women, and would be good to all to come.

But there had now come upon him friendship. Though the particular love had passed and all its habits, friendship remained; and friendship, even to a man so jaded, was a profound thing.

Even as he thus mused he heard the step which was unmistakable, and a particular voice greeting his gentlemen without salutations in the vestibule. That charming voice answered their respect without any insolence and yet with a certain frankness which was properly bred of a great, a thoroughly exalted place now long enjoyed. Then the tall white-and-gilt door was opened—one leaf of it—by a hand delicate and poised, shut at once, and he took her hands.

Now at last he was at home, and for some few minutes the intolerable tedium, the inexorable weight of what life had come to be for him, would be lifted; the voice was enough for that, and the

gestures, and the more than kindness of the face;
the sympathy in everything of the senses, and
common memories apparently unregretted, and
permitting her apparently (he did not deceive
himself, he believed it, though to her it was bitter
enough), a powerful abandonment of the past.

She had all that remains of youth in the beginning of her maturity, which endeared her the
more to him, and an acquiescence in this new relation, in this frank friendship, which yet again
endeared her to him. Yes . . . he was sure . . .
affection was a stronger motive with her than the
mere desire to retain a power in great affairs,
though this she also loved.

That fresh, that musical, that companionable
voice soothed him, supported him, and nourished
him; he was steeped in home.

So those two sat together before that fire, using
little names they had used for so many years;
he receiving what he had never known with any
other—I mean the maternity and the sisterhood
of women, so strongly reinforced by recently
remembered, recently practised love. She alone
could ask him, without his first speaking, whether
he would not remain. (In the kitchens towards
the *Ménage* what courses had she not prepared!)
But the Furies were upon him again, the cold

Furies of the body and of the soul, the Furies of exhausted passions, which led to no end, the Furies of the flesh. He could not rest; he rose again. They had been together twenty minutes. It was enough for him, and he could not think of her save as in relation to himself. Yet was this man not selfish, only cursed; but this curse could not now be lifted. He might once have conjured it away, not so long ago—it was now too late.

The gentlemen in the vestibule drew themselves up as they heard his step, not stiffly, but with just that rectitude which marked the obeisance of great names to their master, and he and she went out, talking almost gaily, to the doors of the coach. He gave her an appointment, not for the morrow, for he had public business that he hated, but for the morrow after, and at Versailles. He needed her advice with the envoys, and she must meet these foreigners. Whereat they smiled at each other. Then went he into his coach, and his gentlemen with him. They drove up to the great iron gates before this little palace; they turned to the right along the road to Versailles.

She went about her business in the house; she

could not help but listen with a part of her mind, strangely detached though it were, to the last clatter of the horses beyond the wall; and neither he nor she understood that the monarchy had been wasted, lost, thrown away.

THE THREE PLACES: FONTAINEBLEAU, MADRID, SARATOGA

(*October* 16, 1777)

THE 16th of October is a date of some import in French annals. On that day Marie Antoinette was killed before her Tuileries gardens. On that day was Wattignies won: "The chief feat of arms of the Republic." On that day also—years before—were done, in three widely distance places, four very different acts; if we see these acts, first each separate, then all combined, they show us the magnitude and the irony of our lives. Sharply do these four acts in these three places illuminate the story of France and of the world.

*   *   *   *   *

For now two years the American colonies of England had been in organized rebellion. The lingering of that war, its distance, its varied and (in the eyes of Europe) petty episodes, had arrested but not determined opinion. The enemies of England had watched it at first with hope, then with anxiety, and at last with tedium. It dragged out; its issue became more and more clear. The rebels all together made up not half the colonists. Their active forces were but a small fraction of the total manhood. Their failure was foredoomed.

The French monarchy (the great but increasingly embarrassed counterweight to the growing power of London) had missed its chance to strike. The issue was now certain: the colonies (already secured through the defeat of the French before Quebec but a few years ago) would now fall back to the English crown. No solid judgment could doubt that. The drama was ending.

The very young King of France—large, lethargic, slow to comprehend and slower to decide—had earned (over and above the effect of such disabilities) the contempt of his immediate servants. It was not for nothing that Louis XVI. was ponderous with German blood. To all this was added a public negligence, for he had (and it was said, could have) no heir. His young queen had entered that road of abrupt, nervous dissipation, had sown that undeserved enmity, which together would lead on to such a close. The whole air of the Court already threatened. The great strains were at work beneath the even ritual and weighted grandeur of what still governed the nation: the brick behind the encrusted marble was giving way.

The end approached; but, before it came, an accident—a side effect—was to arise. It seemed but a divergence at the time. It proved itself, in its conclusion, something almost as large as the revolution itself.

*　　　*　　　*　　　*　　　*

It was Thursday, the 16th of October, in the palace of Fontainebleau. The Court of France had withdrawn thither for the autumn's hunting. Its concern was with its own splendour and with its innumerable personal dramas. No large affair was toward.

The season was benignant, the woods were still gorgeous, the forest beyond the palace was full of fruition and repose; something of a late summer still lingered.

There had been hunting in the rides between the trees that day, but long before sunset the most tardy of the followers had returned, their mud upon them. Evening had come, the horses were stabled, the day's work was long over. The magnificence of the public banquet was extinguished; even the eternal card-playing had tired itself out, and the silence had come. In their distant rooms two separate men began to work alone: each to think in silence before he put pen to paper. One was Vergennes, the other Goltz.

Vergennes, Foreign Minister to the King of France, a man of sixty, tried, careful, covered his face with his hand as he sat and wove within his mind. His every energy had been bent to the undoing of the war which had lost Canada—and much more. He sought an issue and he found none. There had been a moment. . . . There had been a moment. . . . Best when the formal declaration of independence was known in Europe: recoverable that summer when the ships with the American envoys on board had been seen from the British coast. But the moment had passed. . . . He saw no issue. He considered the play of the forces in Europe. He considered the decision of his master, the king. He saw, as in a picture, the fleets and their balanced powers, the prestige, the promptitude of the British admirals. He felt, like the memory of a voice, the hesitation of any king to help rebels in arms. He remembered the way in which the Spanish Court (Bourbons also) had failed them. He feared it would fail them still. Spain would not move. He stirred a moment, as though to rise and seek some paper in a drawer. He lifted his hand from his eyes and blinked at the candle-light. Then he sank back again. Of what purport could it be to find the precise words? His one ally, the Spanish Court, had failed him and would fail him. Perhaps they were right. The American colonies could now claim no friends. Their sovereign was too strong, and, after all, his rule was legitimate. The British would make good at last.

All such meditation done, the man changed his place, pulled his chair up towards the desk, settled his papers, and set him down to write. It was more than deep night. For all the fast shut windows and heavy curtains, one could smell the early morning. There was no sound in the vast house. All slept (he thought) save him. In such a silence and such a darkness he put down his judgment—that the Ministers of George III. now thought themselves independent of the world; that while it was true that the two Bourbon Courts must go warily, yet had he worked hard and felt broken hearted. He paused a moment in his writing, then set down, to guide himself, what was true enough, "He had no wish for war. . . . But neither had he any wish for humiliation. But what should he do if the triumphant British Government demanded of him that he should treat the Americans as outlaws and as pirates?" It was an inconclusive jumble: no more than the fixing of his mind by repetition of what he had written publicly that day. Not often do men of such powers leave work of such sort incomplete. But he left it thus; summoned his servant, who had fallen asleep in the room without, and himself went through the great doors to the inner room to sleep.

In that same night, in another room, far more simply furnished, the envoy of the Prussian king —Goltz—entered, in his precise idiom and hand, another conclusion, which showed how all minds at that instant worked together. He wrote down that the French had had their opportunity and had lost it, and that George III. was now secure in the mastery of the two worlds.

In Madrid, on that same night, Florida Blanca wrote for his master also. He drafted advice, and made a memorandum of the advice he had drafted. It was advice to his colleague of the Court of France. It was a judgment of the King of Spain for his brother Bourbon of France. There was but one thing to be done—regrettable, no doubt, but necessary. Perhaps there had been a chance, but the chance was lost. The immediate, the practical, unquestioned concern of any sane man now was to walk very carefully where Britain was concerned. Everything must be forgone which could even raise complaint from St. James's, for said he to himself, as he rose from this brief exercise and made also himself for his own chamber: "The thing is now settled and history cannot be re-written. It would have been better otherwise, no doubt, but the American Colonies are destined to be British Colonies again, and for ever. All that talk I have heard young men indulge in, of a new State beyond the Atlantic, is young men's talk."

At that phrase he smiled, and in his turn summoned his servants and went to his repose.

* * * * *

But in the woods above the Hudson Valley, on the heights of Saratoga, on that same Thursday, the 16th of October, 1777, a lost body of only four thousand effectives all told, under the British general Burgoyne, with its guns (not three dozen left), had completed its surrender to the colonial levies. And in much those same hours of which I speak, those European midnight hours and hours of the early morning, the late evening of the West had seen this small thing quite completed. A little force, such a force as to-day we might almost put upon a couple of transports, had laid down its arms to an uncertain gathering of irregulars.

And what a consequence!

Some three weeks later a rumour was abroad, no one knew why it came, or how. Another week and men asked why it was that Ministers in England said nothing of the Hudson, and spoke only of successes elsewhere. Moved by we know not what instinct, Vergennes sat him down at last and wrote a note insisting that the new State should be recognized.

It was the 4th of December. Upon the very morrow the full news was known. Upon the 6th the young king—Heaven knows with what hesitation and with what future regrets—put, in his large round hand, at the foot of that document, "Approved." Upon the 8th Franklin and his companions, sitting at Passy, wrote out and signed their acceptance of the French Alliance.

THE END OF CHATEAUBRIAND

(November 27, 1843–July 18, 1848)

CHATEAUBRIAND was in England. He
was at 35 Berkeley Square—a very old man
(he was in his seventy-fifth year), and nearer
the tomb than he knew. His legs, very thin and
feeble, supported him ill. His hands, gouty and
knotted, trembled a little. Even his fine eyes had
lost much of their brilliance. He stooped in his
slow walk, but he was supported by pride. He
had determined to return to England where, fifty
years before, in the eagerness of his young manhood, he had first loved. For of all his unstable,
self-reflecting, unrooted adventures in those affairs, two only left something permanent with
him—one the parson's daughter of his youth in
Bungay, and the other the strong friendship of
his last hours. He returned to the country where
he had been ambassador and in the height of his
fame.

It was the heir of France in exile who had
bidden him come, and it was certainly in loyalty
to the throne—to that immemorial line, to the
institution which was the soul of his country, to

the Capetians—that the old man had made the journey. It was not for memories of Bungay, still less for memories of the Embassy.

It was November—the most lonely month of the year. It was the 27th of that month. Chateaubriand had already been in London three days. The young heir of France in exile, the Comte de Chambord, bade him to that house, giving him for his use all the ground floor (for the great man dared not face stairs, though he still could move), and when, the next day, the prince received, he had himself helped and carried up to the main room, where a crowded mass of curious English, of loyal or interested French, passed before the prince in exile and bowed in turn to him. At the back of that crowd the Comte de Chambord saw, standing with difficulty among the rest in the press, the figure of the man whom he had brought at such a season overseas. He moved towards him at once, vigorously and spontaneously; without care for his own position at the moment; eager to salute the man whose greatness he sincerely recognized, whose usefulness to the throne had been a tradition for that younger generation (the prince was but twenty-three), and whose name was at the moment greater than any other name in France. He took

both his poor gouty hands and said Chateaubriand must not stand. He put a chair for him.
He told him, without flattery, that he depended
upon his presence.

There was no one in that room like him, and
Chateaubriand himself complained how many
French had stayed away from fear—he had also
complained, without reason, that official England
had shunned the exile—there was no one in that
room, I say, but saw two figures supreme among
them: the exile, who later might, if he would,
have been king; and that old man of the laurels,
who knew himself, and was known by all of them
already, to be a sort of immortal—such a pen
had he.

The reception was over, the blaze of candles
extinguished, the old man had been helped back
again to his rooms below. He took paper and,
as best he could with his failing fingers, noted
the points of what next day he must dictate—as
next day he did—to his last friend. Next day
also that long letter was written and remains to
us. It has a phrase upon the Comte de Chambord, upon Henry V., which is not to be forgotten:—

"The kings would have done well to have
saluted this young ghost of a time outworn.

They would have done well not to insult, as he passed, a traveller who had nothing to show but a broken sceptre in his hand. They laughed: they did not see that the world has grown tired of them, and that time will force them at last to take that same road as has been taken by the great royal line which protected them all and lent them a life which fails them now."

*   *   *   *   *

Chateaubriand was in the rue du Bac, in those rooms on the ground floor where he was to end. The great windows opened upon a town garden, dark with trees in spite of the light of July.

His friend, Jeanne Françoise Récamier, was awaiting, herself in old age, ready to join him again.

Everything that he had been, all that had made up himself—his vivacity and changeableness of love, and tenacious hate—seemed to have departed, and he lay as though he had already fallen into the power of death, though his eyes still shone. He heard, but with difficulty. He spoke hardly at all, and then in but few, murmuring words. Over his paralysed body they had thrown a coverlet, upon which his hands lay still. He was waiting for the advent of the friend whose friendship alone remained to him of life. But she herself, who had been the most famous of beautiful women as he had been the most famous of lyrical men, had come also to the term of things; and those eyes of hers, which had held captive a generation, were now nearly blind. As he so lay, awaiting her, there returned to his weakened mind a certain phrase of his own writing not so long before, where he had spoken of human affection and had said of love that time changes our hearts as it does our complexion and our years. Nevertheless there is one exception amid all this infirmity of human things, for it does come about sometimes that in some strong soul one love lasts long enough to be transformed into a passionate friendship, to take on the qualities of duty, and almost those of virtue. Then does love lose the decadence of our nature and lives on, supported by an immortal principle.

She to whom—or rather, round whom—those words were written was brought in, a ghost of the past, as he was a ghost of the past, to sit by him as he lay there, silent and deafened, on the edge of death. There could pass very little between them. They had neither of them the strength to speak at any length: nor she in a voice which he could well hear, nor he in a voice strong enough to reach her ears. But her presence was a final consolation.

When she left him after that singular interval of communion and silence he slept a little, and the next day he knew that his end had come.

It was Sunday, the 2nd of July. Outside, in the streets, the noise of the popular revolt had hardly died down, and contrasted with that too great energy of sound and of young fury was this silent room opening upon the garden, and the figure lying there. He asked in a whisper for the Sacraments—he who had said in a phrase which showed the man like lightning: "No Christian believes as I do, nor is any man more sceptical than I."

On the next day, Monday, the 3rd, his life still dragged on and diminished, yet he whispered to his nephew, who took down the words from his lips: "I declare before God my retraction of all there may be in my writings contrary to the Faith, to good morals, and in general to the principles which are conservative of good." And his nephew put down beneath those lines: "Signed for my uncle, whose hand can no longer sign." He had the declaration read to him; he tried to read it with his own failing eyes. Yet another night dragged on; but it was not until Tuesday, the 4th, that he died, and there had come back to that death-bed the friend, the old woman—Madame Récamier. Besides her there was but his nephew, his confessor, and a Sister of Charity. It was a little after eight in the morning. The priest and the Sister of Charity were kneeling at the end of the bed; the two others stood and saw his passing.

So he died.

*   *   *   *   *

A fortnight later, upon Tuesday, July 18, 1848, they brought the body of Chateaubriand for burial to the place which he had chosen. That insecure, moving, intense soul of his was steeped in its own time, thinking that sublime which to-day we think grotesque, and which to-morrow our descendants may think sublime again. He had determined, in his passion for things both singular and glorious, in his vanity, but also in his love of greatness, upon a peculiar tomb, and it was now to receive him.

The Cathedral of Saint Malo was filled with the sailors of the place, with peasants come in from the countryside, with the clergy of the province, with all the officials of the town and even of Rennes—a vast crowd. They laid the coffin in the Chapel of the Sacred Heart, blazing with candles, and all that afternoon and all night long the crowd kept pouring in to pass by this lying-in-state and to pray, in a stream that did not end hour after hour.

On the next day, the Wednesday after the last Mass to be said over him, the runners harnessed the horses, and the whole train set out for that rock which is an island at high tide and in which his tomb had been cut. It had been placed for him alone, and he had ordered—a last singularity—that there should be no name or inscription upon it whatsoever. As they laid him in his tomb the guns sounded a last salute, the walls of the city were covered with men and women watching that strange sight, and even the rocks to seaward and along the shore were black with people. They say that fifty thousand stood by and saw the sight.

And there he is to-day; and no one can say at all whether, with the passage of time, he who was at that moment the greatest of the great will become greater still, or insignificant.

A SOLDIER OF '70

(*June* 1870)

IN the height of a scorching summer, in June 1870, a young man, tall, lean, long in features, active in gesture, something fanatical, with deep-set and fixing eyes, pushed a perambulator (of all things!) along a pavement of the South Bank in Paris. By his side was the mother of the child: nor was she his wife.

I have said "young man," but in years he was a boy. He was but twenty years old. That household he had set up was a curious adventure indeed. His parents, as he thought, knew nothing of it; and perhaps he was right. The strict laws of the French family would have forbidden a marriage. But his allowance was sufficient and his happiness was complete. At that age one is immortal; and as he lived in an undefeated society at the height of its hope and wealth, as he had himself hope and wealth beneath him in the largest measure for his foundation, nothing mattered but the intensity of his affection in this opening of his life.

There he was, in this comically small domestic

manner, at the summit of whatever this life can bring, and trusting rightly to chance for the regulation of all things.

It was, I say, in the middle of that burning summer, and if the foreign affairs of the country were talked of at all (after small but supposedly splendid foreign victories), they were for him and his like but newspaper talk. They did not touch realities between waking and sleeping.

There was this difference between him and his like—that he had in him a certain material which could catch fire, and having caught fire would blaze unfed until he should die.

Ten weeks later this young man, or boy, having volunteered, was on the field of Sedan. The capitulation was announced; the men were already beginning to pile arms, and he, by a chance, was arguing with certain bearers who were moving a body. They maintained that the man was dead; he said that he was alive. He had his way, and he proved right. This also was a sharp point in his life, which he remembered always, even more clearly than any other episode of that disaster: how, while it was yet full light, he had argued with the bearers. The man whom he had saved he kept close to years after, making

him a friend; for they went off as prisoners together into the Germanies.

That young man broke prison, and found his
way to the Rhine and farther. He spoke no
German; he did but ask his way; and when he
had reached his own country again he went to
the nearest centre and re-enlisted.

They sent him to the Loire. All this while he
had heard nothing from his own people, or from
what was nearer to him than his own people.
So he served through that memorable and terrible winter under Chanzy, and saw the failure to
relieve the capital. In those snows he came of
age.

He did not see Paris again until he came there
with the rank of captain in the troops of Thiers,
for the suppression of the Commune. It was
against one of the last barricades, near the foot
of the Northern Hill, that he received his third
wound in all that fighting, national and civil. To
his old age he remembered that scene as a com-
edy for all its slaughter. He saw himself something of a chromo-lithograph, waving a sword
and leading his men, who were Bretons. He
turned his face toward the barricade, and at that
moment saw, peering between two stones, the
face of a boy younger than himself—a boy in no

uniform, with a bandolier slung over the blue
canvas of his blouse. He saw the boy's musket
resting on the stones and pointed towards him.
He remembered that it was singularly fore-
shortened . . . and almost in the same instant
that he saw this thing he felt as though a horse
had kicked him with full strength on the left
arm. He fell down, stunned, without pain; but
a very few moments afterwards, as they carried
him back, the pain grew intolerable. It was the
worst thing he had suffered in all those months,
and it was a day before the confusion of his
thoughts relaxed. When his mind grew slowly
clear again, he saw (more vividly than the dirty
walls of the gaunt ward in which he lay) the
barricade, and the boy in the blue canvas, and the
fore-shortened barrel.

*   *   *   *   *

All these enormous things had run their course,
and reached a settlement: the empire gone,
Prussia supreme, the nation half murdered—a
stillness and bitterness over everything. That
which had been his life such a very little time
before had ceased for him altogether. Some who
read this would know too well whom I mean if I
were to give the details of his misfortune, or of

how he followed, but only at a distance, and supported his child: of how he learnt that the mother had left him for ever.

Note this strange thing: that to this young man, even now not yet in his twenty-third year, the torrents of violent emotion had settled into a sort of lake; a permanent feeling, profound, unchangeable, nourishing an unvarying output of appeal. Whatever he had lived, in whatever ways, his own small concealed home, his family for a moment estranged, his tradition and his proud name—all these had distilled into a lyrical patriotism, the fruits of which seemed at first more than half contemptible to the hard French temper about him. Those fruits took many forms. In the first place, he expended his whole self in a perpetual and open insistence upon the necessity for raising the nation against its conqueror; and this he did in a society where all such open and direct expression is greeted as insufficient and unworthy.

He acted thus, ingenuous and direct, in the midst of a Paris and of a France especially bent upon reserve, and he maintained that form of expression in spite of a much ridiculing and, what wounded him more, a patronizing affection. Through all his youth, through all his manhood, on into his middle age and to the verge of old age, this exalted mood affected him to verse, most of it of the second-rate sort; all of it rhetorical; all of it sincere. You may guess how this popular versifying jarred on the critical French ear and soul.

There was no occasion during thirty years, during forty years, in which he did not make it his business to preach continually the duty of reassertion and of warring down a conqueror who had become now assured in strength and rooted, and of whose achievement and mastery there seemed at last no question. It was the moment when Renan said: "France is dying. Let us not brawl at her death-bed."

Long after Alsace-Lorraine had become mere names to a younger generation which knew nothing of the war, through mighty civil contests of opinion and even of religion (which the French alone wage in our time), his simple note sounded continually: at first acclaimed by the poor; always ridiculed by the too-cultured or the too-fatigued: latterly almost grotesque, still sounding in a world which had completely changed. In some part of his expression he had aged prematurely. In body he was still alert, though his last illness was upon him; in the vigour of his gesture, the fire of his glance, he was more than he had ever been.

By the year 1912—so oddly do human things turn about in the short unit of one lifetime—his career, his verse, his rhetoric, his perpetual insistence, had become a sort of institution for the nation. Societies love to take those of an older generation and to make them symbols. Even his literary insufficiency was half forgiven, and men talked of him as a sort of curious relic from the days when war was possible, and when the glory of a national rehabilitation (now impossible) could be reasonably entertained. But with this position of his among his fellow-citizens (which was quaintly mixed up with the love we bear for ancient things, almost because they are odd, and largely because we are sure they can never return) there now went something of grandeur. He was now, they said, an old man; and his very insistence in harping upon so single and so unfertile a theme had given him his definite place. And just as men would say, "So and so is now our great poet, So and so our great actor, So and so this, and So and so that," in the same way they pointed to the man now grown old and said, "He, of course, is our great patriot," but they said it with a smile. One man, however, who loved him, called him "Tyrtæus": quizzically enough, I think.

No one thought it possible that his war would come.

His illness grew upon him fast. By one of those accidents which show the lives of men to be ordered, as the parts of an actor are ordered upon the stage, this man died just in those days before the war, when it was far too late for any man to remember great wars in Western Europe as a reality, and still some weeks too early for men to have grown uneasy and to think they already heard the guns. But as though so simple, so direct, and so very great a life were a presage, his funeral made a great picture.

There was a sort of silence after his death, like that which comes before a storm. Nor was the moment long delayed.

Upon a certain day, memorable to all of us, the Cabinet of Berlin presented a brief note to the Government of Paris. Prussia would fight in the East, and demanded as a guarantee the frontier garrisons of the French, over and above a promise of neutrality. We know the reply, and we know what followed.

The first young men to cross the frontier in arms (which was in the pine forests on the crests of the Vosges) pulled up the frontier post for a trophy. There was no discussion as to what should be done with that trophy. The decision seemed inevitable. It was sent back to be set upon this man's grave, and there I saw it the other day. It had been set up hurriedly, and was leaning a little sideways. It always remains in my mind as the most significant monument in Europe. The grave is in a small cemetery upon the country hills which lie to the west of Paris, a cemetery so domestic and of such small consequence to the little village it belongs to that no good road leads to it, but the dead of the village are brought up from the main road a quarter of a mile off by bearers who follow a rough track.

Up this track, with a ritual dear to the French people, did certain delegates bear that frontier post, as we bear dead men for whom we proclaim the resurrection. They took it through the rustic gate into that small, neglected place, and put it upon the grave of the man who had lived so strange and inartistic a life: who stirred, and was gladdened in his sleep.

TWO MEN OF THE MARNE

(*September* 9, 1914)

IT was a little after five in the afternoon of
Wednesday, 9th September, when a general
officer with the Ninth French Army rode with
one companion up the road from Sezanne. He
had clearly in his mind on a landscape map the
memory of three disastrous days just past. He
saw the line upon that map like a small, vivid
picture; he saw it as it was also in reality—the
crushing of his centre back and back, day after
succeeding day, through the Sunday, the Monday,
the Tuesday, and the early hours of this the
Wednesday, in which the crisis had come: the
crisis of the Marne.

To the north the ceaseless noise of the guns
which had filled those four days still rolled, and
as he heard it he considered the 42nd Division.
It had just arrived behind the gap opening between the 11th and the 9th Corps. To his right,
and also to the northward, but behind the line of
the battle, a great storm-cloud was growing to
cover the sky, and beneath it, where it darkened
the last brilliance of that intensely hot day, the

sharp edge of the Champagne hills, the steep down near the marshes of St. Gond, and the strangely isolated height of the Mont Aimé stood out unnaturally clear, the latter with the western light of the declining sun full on it against the ominous livid purple of the thunder-cloud. At its base the Prussian Guard had stretched out to the limit of their numbers; they were already too far extended; they were still advancing. Behind again to the right (he did not know in what confusion, but the confusion had come) bunched the Saxons.

That vast modern battle was not one in which, as in those of our fathers' time, the decisive moment was grasped by the eye, and the decisive manœuvre conducted upon a field actually seen by the man deciding it. In that vast modern battle the critical moment was the end of calculation infinitely complex and stretching back for days; yet there was, in this moment of the late afternoon, on that Wednesday, essentially the same process maturing in a length of days which had with the great Napoleon matured in an hour; and what was about to be done was essentially the same as what Marlborough had done at Blenheim, when he drew that heavy phalanx of white-coated German cavalry from the right, under the heights, and launched it at the French left centre and decided Blenheim; for the enemy line, though still advancing, was stretched to its utmost, was breaking: the gap in the German line had been perceived, and proved fatal to the Germans.

The general officer returned from his ride a little after six o'clock. He sat in the room of a private house, which during the last twenty-four hours had been the conning tower of the fight. He had the great map before him, scored with rough chalk. He saw through the tall windows before him the lowering sky. He received minute by minute the telephone messages, and marked their news in sharp pencil jabs upon the sheet. The dull noise to the north was the same; the reports pouring in from the front showed little change, but that little change was as significant as the slight movement after slack water in a harbour, when the tide begins to turn.

It was still full daylight; the storm had broken on those northern hills; there were lightning flashes against the dead cloud, and the noise of distant thunder mingled with the ceaseless thudding of the guns. The general ceased his labour and could lean back in his chair, resting his eyes from the map, and make certain that the thing was accomplished. An order had been given upon the enemy's side, and it was an order for retreat. . . .

The evening fell, the rain drove through darkness, the thunder lessened, grumbled and withdrew. None slept. All followed the more distant, the withdrawing signal of the artillery. The reserve troops came marching through, hurrying to the north. The tide had indeed turned.

The general offcer was mounted again with his few companions and riding north with the rest through the storm. Before midnight a great glare was seen on the horizon, blurred with rain. He informed himself what it was, and heard it was the station of La Fére Champenoise burning: the enemy had abandoned it three hours before. And still they went northwards, and still the far noise of the guns retired before them, miles away.

*   *   *   *   *

There is a house in Luxembourg built for a large school and standing upon the public square opposite the post office. Here was housed, in that same September of 1914, the Central Command of the German armies. Hence proceeded the central determining orders which moulded the battle reaching along one hundred and fifty miles of front, two hundred miles away.

The little hill-town on its splendid gorge was quiet enough. The German officers came and went through the streets, courteous, not ill-liked, among a people whom they had always regarded as one of their own; no cruelties had marked this violation of what they thought to be no more than a technical neutrality. The coinage, the customs, the railways had been German for a lifetime; German speech was all about them, and the traditions they knew. The afternoon was fair and warm in Luxembourg, high though the town stands. Here was all the odd, ironic air of peace, though here was the heart of the attack and of the enormous war.

Into that great empty building, now filled with its busy groups of writing and telephoning men, its big, bare deal tables with their masses of maps pinned down, its walls covered with further maps, lines in blue and red chalk drawn upon them and numbers hastily inscribed, came for the first time, after so many days of triumphant advance, the note of change. There was half an hour of too great calm, during which decision wrestled against decision and a proud refusal to accept inevitable things; but the moment came; it was the reflex of that same moment, a little after five o'clock, when the thunderstorm had broken far away beyond the reedy belts of the Marne River. An order had been given at the front: the man upon whose responsibility it went—a man already broken with illness—rose and went out uncertainly, as though he were far older than his age, leaning upon the plain iron rail of the school staircase as he painfully descended the steps; then slowly, with bent head, wandered into the neglected court and garden.

Between him and the public square there was but a low wall supporting high, open rails far apart. He came in his full uniform, this general officer, who had accepted and ordered the retirement. He was a nobleman, superior in military talent to his fellows, even amid that great organization, which was the best designed for war in Europe. He leaned against the railings a moment with his left hand, his whole body was bowed, and then he sat him down, careless of dignity, careless of prestige. He sat down publicly on the low stone wall that supported the railings, his head bending more and more forward, and staring on the ground. He bore a name with very different memories of cold triumph. It was Moltke.

A group of boys playing in the square ceased from play to gaze at the old boy, timidly approached the railings, and stared at that poor, broken figure. They could know nothing of the traditions of the Prussian army, nor of how strange a sight they saw, but they felt its enormity. He, for his part, had forgotten what was around him—the place, the children; he stared at the ground, remembering as in a vivid dream his urgent appeal to his emperor, his agony at defeat, his intelligence too great for his heart, and the knell still ringing there: "The campaign has failed. . . . The campaign has failed."

THE END